VERMONT
TOWNSCAPE

VERMONT TOWNSCAPE

by

Norman Williams, Jr.
Edmund H. Kellogg
Peter M. Lavigne

CENTER
FOR URBAN
POLICY RESEARCH

Published by the Center for Urban Policy Research
Building 4051—Kilmer Campus
New Brunswick, New Jersey 08903

Library of Congress Cataloging-in-Publication Data

Williams, Jr., Norman, 1915-
  Vermont townscape.

  Includes bibliographical references.
  1. Historic districts—Vermont—Conservation and
restoration.   2. Central business districts—Vermont—
Conservation and restoration.   3. Architecture—Vermont—
Conservation and restoration.   I. Kellogg, Edmund Halsey,
1912-   .   II. Lavigne, Peter M.   III. Rutgers
University.   Center for Urban Policy Research.
IV. Title.
NA730.V4W5   1986   363.6'9'09743   86-17550
ISBN 0-88285-120-9

Excerpts from *The City in History*, Copyright © 1961 by Lewis Mumford, are reprinted here by permission of Harcourt Brace Jovanovich, Inc. Excerpts from *The Making of Urban America*, Copyright © 1965 by John W. Reps, are reprinted by permission.

Production by Mary A. Picarella, assisted by Arlene H. Pashman.

Table of Contents

Acknowledgments

On behalf of the Environmental Law Center of the Vermont Law School, we present herewith our findings on an important problem—what is the essence of Vermont townscape?

To our great good fortune, the Cecil Howard Charitable Trust took an interest in the question of exactly what it is that makes Vermont towns so special and gave us a substantial grant to explore Vermont Townscape. Robert Sincerbeaux, director of the Trust, has taken a vital and active part throughout. We are grateful to the group of remarkable consultants who have contributed so much to this project. Professor Wilhelm von Moltke has been able to give us a great deal of help, sharpening our perspective on urban design along with wise counsel on all sorts of matters.

In addition, several of the leading experts in their particular fields have given generously of their expertise, particularly in helping to set us off in the right direction at the start. These include Professor John W. Reps of Cornell, on the historical background of American urban planning; the late Professor Kevin Lynch of the Massachusetts Institute of Technology, on how people visualize the structure of urban development; Ronald Fleming of the Townscape Institute, on all the myriad details of New England townscape; Professor Jere Daniell of Dartmouth, on the origin of the current image of Vermont towns and the extent of its historical validity; President Nicholas Muller of Colby-Sawyer College, on Vermont history in general; and the late Bryan Lynch and the late Charles Helmer, on the local tradition in landscape architecture and architecture.

It goes without saying that we have appreciated deeply the extensive support from Vermont Law School and its Environmental Law Center. Thanks are due to present and past administrative assistants at the Environmental Law Center, Leslie Staudinger and Ulla Virks, for their patience with the extensive bookkeeping and the myriad of other details of the project. Special thanks to Nina Thomas for her many hours of labor on the manuscript and her many memos.

No academic venture can be much better than the work of its student assistants, and we have been fortunate in those who have worked with us on these materials. Among those who have made special efforts have been Chase van Gorder, Tom Hoban, Bill Taylor, Sue Danielson, Susan Kidd, and Nancy Gordon on the original collection of materials, and Robert Smith, Ken Briggs, Maxine Grad, Bob Miller, Tim Richards, Alison Gravel, Jenny Carter, and Karen Christensen on various intermediate projects. Thanks are also due to the fine photographers whose works grace the book.

To state the obvious, although all the individuals mentioned have made contributions, none can be charged with any of the detailed conclusions, which are the exclusive responsibility of the authors.

Finally, the many important contributions of Professor Richard O. Brooks, director of the Environmental Law Center, cannot go without mention. His comments, critiques, and commitment kept the project alive at critical junctures, and Vermont Townscape would not have been completed without him.

Norman Williams, Jr.
Edmund H. Kellogg
Peter M. Lavigne

The Old Bennington Church

JOAN LIGHTFOOT

The Special Value of New England Townscape

If the Spanish colonial town in the New World was a military survival, the New England village was a happy mutation. In the settlement of the Back Bay colony, the Puritan adventurers, though they were more familiar with trade and handicraft than farming, easily resisted the temptation to pile up their population in the port of Boston. Fortunately, they were dependent at the beginning upon agriculture, and this forced them to risk spreading their plantations thinly, in order to occupy the land. The heart of their new towns and villages was the Common: an open area, often larger than the Spanish plaza, where their sheep and cattle might safely graze, under the eye of a municipal official, the cattle reeve. Around the common, from the very outset, the public buildings were erected: the meeting house, the town hall, and later the school. These institutions served as a rallying point for the community, and the Common did duty as drill ground for the local militia: another medieval institution. The medieval ideal of self-government, so imperfectly fulfilled in Europe on account of the persistent opposition by lords, bishops, bourgeois magnates, here came into full flower, for the Protestant congregation had control of the church as well as the town.

Each member of the community at the beginning was allotted his share of the land: usually from half an acre to an acre within the village, though the parson might have as much as ten acres, while the farm allotments lay in the outskirts, beyond the early stockades, sometimes far enough to justify the erection of a summer house, as in the medieval city. In the early regulations, according to William Weeden, no one was permitted to live more than half a mile from the meeting house lest, in the rigors of a New England winter, he should evade his social obligations as a member of the Church.

Sometimes the common was a wide strip of a hundred and fifty or two hundred feet, running the length of the village, as in Sharon, Connecticut, sometimes an oblong or a square. Around this area, from the eighteenth century on, were set the separate houses, with white clapboards and green shutters, free standing, decently separated from their neighbors, with deep rear gardens large enough for a small orchard and a stable, as well as a vegetable plot. Tall elm trees or maples on each side of the road furnished shade from the torrid summer sun and partial windbreaks against the winter wind; their leafy arcade unified the scattered houses: a perfect unison of man and nature. . . .

Each family had its rights in the common land; each family had fields on the outskirts, as well as gardens nearer their homes; each male had the duty of participating in the political affairs of the town through the annual town meeting. A democratic polity—and the most healthy and comely kind of environment, as long as it remained on a small scale. . . . Today one looks with a fresh eye on all these mutations: especially the seventeenth-century Dutch village and New England village: both expressions of a new kind of dynamic ecological balance, superior to either the urban monopolies of the Middle Ages or the unregulated sprawl, industrial or suburban, that followed. As in the penetrating psychology of a Spinoza or a Rembrandt we find a spirit more available for the future than in the sharp mechanical analysis of a Descartes or the more typical portraiture of the court painters like van Dyck, so in these urban forms we find an early empirical anticipation of the pattern for a dynamically balanced environment, urban and rural, like that we must eventually create in terms of our own culture, for a whole civilization.

Lewis Mumford, *The City in History*

One fact remains clear: the stereotype image of the New England village with its lofty meetinghouse spire rising from a crisply painted, green-shuttered building fronting a central green and dominating a cluster of large, comfortable "colonial" houses does not fairly represent conditions during the early years of settlement. The grace and charm of the New England were long in the making. These were pioneer communities. Some, like Windsor, Connecticut, in 1637 began as small fortress stockades enclosing a square of dwellings that were little more than huts. In others, such as Salem, the first places of residence were tiny dugouts scooped out of a bank or were bark-covered sapling-framed shelters built in imitation of Indian dwellings. Even the surviving larger houses from the middle and late seventeenth century, with their unpainted plank or clapboard siding and their small windows, bear witness to the stern requirements of a frontier existence. In many of the early settlements it was not until nearly half a century or so after original settlement that the architectural qualities we associate with the New England community began to take form. . . .

Close study of these town plans leads inescapably to the conclusion that the very real visual distinction of the New England village stems less from the merits of their two-dimensional plans than from the combination of buildings and plant materials that developed by semi-accident many years after their layout. Perhaps this merely proves that simple plans often adapt best to changing circumstance. So while the plans were simple but varied, it is the third dimension of the villages that is cherished. The scale, the materials, the architectural designs inherited from abroad but modified to meet the new environment—all combined with the village layout to produce a total quality of community that has yet to be equalled in America except in isolated towns of outstanding character.

John W. Reps, *The Making of Urban America*

Introduction

WHAT IS TOWNSCAPE?

The elegant yet understated New England town is one of our most readily identifiable cultural attributes. The photographs of *Yankee* and *Vermont Life* and the "shot heard 'round the world" on Lexington Common form integral parts of our cultural history and landscape. In the dense forests that surround small towns in today's Vermont, the church spires, inns, and commons serve as the functional focal point of the human landscape.

Vermont's "townscape"—in particular, the dwindling numbers of picture-perfect, unspoiled villages—is one of the state's most precious assets. By "townscape" is meant the overall visual impression of a town—the total impression it makes on a resident or visitor. Townscape reflects the familiar principle that the whole is greater than the sum of its parts: the overall impression has a life of its own beyond its constituent parts— the *tout ensemble*, as they say in New Orleans.[1] Nevertheless, the whole consists of its various parts; if certain attractive elements recur regularly and dominate the landscape, then it may be assumed that these are of the essence.

WHY PROTECT?

The obvious question must be faced at the outset: why this concern with scenic values in general and Vermont townscape in particular? The first and obvious answer is that attractive townscape gives pleasure to a lot of people: they like it and tend to regard it as rather important in the quality of life. In fact, beautiful townscape is a principal reason why people come to Vermont and why natives stay. More, though, is involved than just a sensitive preference on the part of those few who spend time thinking seriously about aesthetic matters. If anyone has doubts on this point, just listen to the reaction of residents anywhere in Vermont to a proposal to plow a highway through town—or count the number of tourist buses in an attractive town during foliage season. The problem of protecting beautiful townscape arises, in fact, only because such townscape has so broad an appeal.

Much more is involved here, however, than a sense of pleasure in one of the amenities of life. The most attractive towns clearly differ from what they were in the initial years of settlement, yet they still represent genuine survivals of at least some aspects of the historic past. To the extent that this is true, they serve to teach in a vivid way an important aspect of history—how Vermonters used to live. Social history is far more real to those who have a chance to look at some of the major historic artifacts, so that past history can be visualized against the appropriate physical background. An awareness of our historical roots may be important in a period of rapid change and considerable confusion, really as a perspective on ourselves.

In addition, the older buildings in these towns preserve an architectural heritage far superior to much of the rather dreary current development. Moreover, town centers, and particularly town commons, have certain permanent values: they give a sense of orientation and identity, as well as providing a principal area for community life and community interaction.

Vermont townscape is also valuable from a quite different angle—as a major part of the economic base of the state. Tourism is now second only to manufacturing in providing income to Vermonters, far surpassing the returns from agriculture. Clearly, these visitors do not come all the way to Vermont to look at the Barre-Montpelier Road or Shelburne Road running south from Burlington. What brings them are the lovely, peaceful landscape and the attractive towns. The point is widely recognized; indeed, the Vermont motel interests took an active part fifteen years ago in pushing through the legislature the state law to abolish billboards—a striking example of enlightened self-interest.

THREE WAYS OF SEEING

The predominant view in magazine photographs is a view of the quintessential Vermont village from afar, usually from an approaching road or one of the nearby hillsides. The white steeple of the Congregational Church stands out clearly, and other buildings are scattered among tall trees.

Another and different image is that of the town and its surrounding hillsides as seen from its streets, usually with special emphasis on the older, central area "downstreet." In these two images, quite different perspectives play an important role, and quite different protective devices would be appropriate. For example, in the image from the hillside, the most important task involves keeping open at least some areas on the hillsides to provide a view of the town below. It is, however, the image of the town center and its surroundings that is primarily emphasized in this book, since that is what both residents and tourists normally look at.

A third view of Vermont towns focuses upon their edges—the (often-expanding) outer rim of the built-up area along the major approach roads to town. Obviously, the first close-up view of a town provides one important definition of its character and may leave a lasting impression upon a visitor.

HISTORICAL VALIDITY OF THE IMAGE

The typical image of New England townscape, specifically with the more attractive, smaller, and older Vermont towns, is not always historically valid. In some circles, these towns are thought of as "the typical colonial town," and much attention can be devoted to restoring the "colonial atmosphere." (This is known among preservationists as "earlying it up.") Others are thought of as typical old, rural farm towns. These views, in many cases, are historically inaccurate. Currently evolving Vermont land and townscape are different in form and content from the colonial and early nineteenth-century ones. For that matter, few buildings dating from the colonial period still exist in Vermont. Extensive settlement by people of European background—and so, permanent buildings—began only a few years before the American Revolution, so "colonial" is almost always a misnomer.

Most of the beautiful Vermont towns involved here grew rapidly from the end of the eighteenth century through the first three or four decades of the nineteenth century. At that time, those settlements looked rather different from the present, rather prettied-up version. The best Vermont townscape now available represents only certain aspects of historical reality. Early nineteenth-century architecture and town planning paid particular respect to the arrangement of buildings and open spaces to fit then-current living patterns, together with the cultural patterns associated therewith. Perhaps more to the point, these patterns primarily reflect the life of that time's equivalent of a local urban elite. Moreover, the image has changed through time.[2]

According to what evidence we have, these towns were frequently in a rather messy condition early in the nineteenth century, which is hardly surprising for a group of brand new towns on a frontier. At times, the town common was closer to a town dump. There was constant encroachment on the common by wagon traffic going across, and often some commercial and even industrial development nearby. (Many town centers were located in order to use water power from the rivers for small industries.) The gradual improvement of the commons and the surrounding environment began roughly with the romantic movement in the early- to mid-nineteenth century. By the 1920s, Vermont townscape began to pick up remarkably, with better maintenance and the disappearance of less attractive development.[3]

Much of what people regard as the typical Vermont town is really based on rather selective photography, as illustrated in almost any issue of *Vermont Life* or in the works of Samuel Chamberlain, author of innumerable picture books and calendars on New England. Neither of these gives much of an idea of factory chimneys or of townscape in mud season. Thus, various motives have played a role in the gradual upgrading of Vermont townscape:[4] patriotism, civic pride, the desire to escape from the cities to a simpler life, and more than a little Chamber of Commerce puffery.

Chelsea and the North Common from the hillside west

TOM HOBAN

The north side of Woodstock Green. Note that all the houses are Federal style and are compatible.

Sign clutter at the approach to Manchester Village

The Vermont townscape with which we are concerned thus represents a combination of various elements. Most of the buildings, and most of the pattern of buildings and open spaces, date from the early nineteenth century. However, some substantial later changes have, on the whole, improved the towns' appearance. The present townscape has more historical validity as a representation of the best period rather than as a representation of the earliest.

The "traditional" character of many Vermont towns is now seriously threatened by invasion from nearby metropolitan areas. As a result, a number of towns have taken various steps to protect themselves against the unhappy events that may (and often do) occur. The approach to this problem is generally phrased in vague terms, e.g., how to protect and enhance their "historic character." Usually, no one has thought through precisely what is meant by protecting "historic character." Which characteristics are historically important and need protection? Which are aesthetically important and also need protection? It is difficult to be confident about protecting something if one doesn't know exactly what that something is.

Accordingly, this book focuses, first, on defining the essential factors involved in the historical and aesthetic character of Vermont towns and, second, on how to protect and enhance these factors. This work is based upon an analysis of thirty towns in the state (see Map 1). The list was developed essentially by consensus—making a tentative list, checking it with knowledgeable people throughout the state, and reviewing it extensively in the field. Formulation of this list is not intended to suggest that all towns listed are "better" than all other towns in Vermont.[5] While the list does contain all the aesthetically finest towns, inevitably, there is room for difference of opinion at the margin. As in most studies, the final number was, to some extent, arbitrary. The list is, however, a representative one—recognizing, for example, such factors as geographic diversity within the state.

This detailed analysis of a large and representative group of the better towns should serve to bring out those recurring common elements that provide the amenity in these towns and others. The towns discussed herein[6] are therefore those that retain some substantial resemblance to the earliest permanent settlements back in the early nineteenth century—or, to put it more precisely, those that represent the current image of how those towns looked.

Speaking generally, the first two types of views discussed above have retained much of their traditional character, but the approaches have sometimes been taken up with ribbon commercial development—development indistinguishable, except perhaps in scale, from the approaches to Newark, Santa Fe, or Peoria. It is the fight to save the towns from this creeping suburbia that inspired this book, *Vermont Townscape*.[7]

Map 1. The Thirty Towns

Notes

1. The phrase was invoked by the Louisiana court upholding (and broadly construing) the constitutional amendment involving the Vieux Carre in *New Orleans* v. *Pergament*, 198 La. 852, 5 So. 2d 129 (1941). The Supreme Court went all out for such aesthetic regulation (in a case not involving that question) in *Berman* v. *Parker*, 348 U.S. 26 (1954).

2. Of course, if the present image is drastically different from the earlier one, then the argument on social history—How did people live in the past?—loses its validity.

3. The change in attitude has been reflected in both periodical literature and fiction. Perry D. Westbrook, in *The New England Town in Fact and Fiction* (1982), discusses the shifting nature of popular images. Magazines like *Yankee* and *Vermont Life* often reflect modern romanticizing.

4. The parallel to Williamsburg is obvious; as has often been pointed out, Williamsburg is modern WASP history. (Where are the slave quarters? What about the paved parking lots?)

5. Three other types of Vermont towns, while they contain a great deal of interest, involve quite different problems and so are not covered herein. Some of the larger towns (really small cities) have areas of appearance and quality comparable to the smaller towns analyzed here. Montpelier and St. Johnsbury are obvious examples. However, in these larger towns, the best areas of townscape are part of the larger whole and so are interrelated in many ways with other features of the towns, so that the problems presented are basically different in kind from those in the smaller towns. (For example, the commercial pattern is necessarily totally different.)

After long discussion, it was decided to omit a group of other towns (Brattleboro and Bellows Falls are good examples) that have an interesting historic character, essentially nineteenth-century industrial and commercial in nature, with a good deal of Victorian architecture mostly in attached buildings—but without the open feeling and the extraordinary visual amenity of the smaller towns. Without in any way suggesting that these towns are less important, the problems involved are quite different and would bear separate analysis.

Our concern here is on towns and villages, i.e., small, concentrated settlements. Of course, some of the most attractive townships in Vermont have no such settlements. Pomfret is an obvious example, with open hillsides and scattered farms and houses. Scenic protection in such towns is an important problem but, again, quite a different one.

6. The thirty towns (see Map 1) finally selected are: Old Bennington, Brandon, Brookfield, Chelsea, Chester, Craftsbury Common, Danville, Dorset, East Poultney, Grafton, Guildhall, Hyde Park, Manchester, Middletown Springs, Montgomery, Newbury, Newfane, Norwich, Orwell, Peacham, Peru, Plymouth, Randolph Center, South Royalton, South Woodstock, Stowe, Strafford, Thetford Hill, Weston, and Woodstock.

7. While *Vermont Townscape* has focused on Vermont for the obvious reason of convenience of access, the method of analysis and many of the conclusions would be generally the same all over New England—except that the mountain backdrop, nearly universal in Vermont, would be less in evidence.

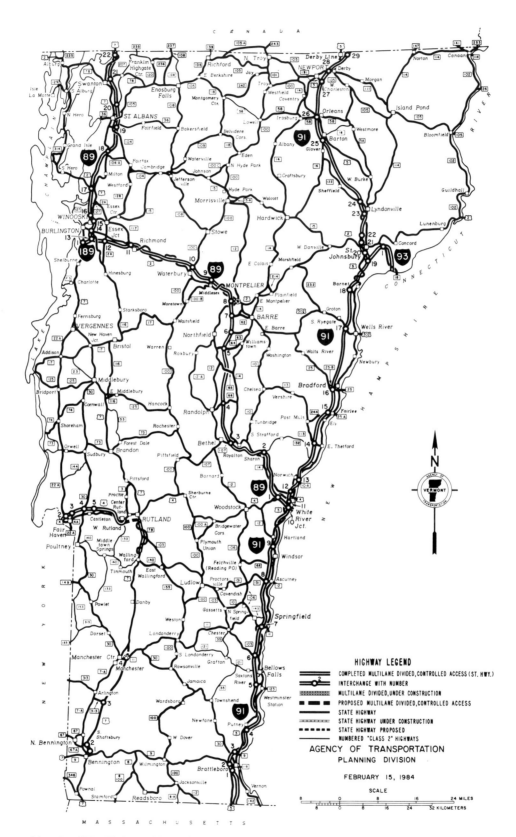

Map 2.   The Highway Network

Chapter 1

The Context of Change in Vermont

The second half of the twentieth century in northern New England is obviously a period of transition: the long-familiar appearance has begun to change rapidly, and so have many of the long-familiar ways. These changes have already had a marked impact on Vermont landscape in general and on townscape in the traditional villages. Some of the most important current trends affecting landscape and townscape derive primarily from forces outside the state; others reflect internal factors, and still others are a combination of the two.

INFLUENCES FROM OUTSIDE

Vermont is situated near the northern end of a broad historic "green belt," now caught between two long ribbons of metropolitan development that are both growing rapidly. "Megalopolis" runs along the Atlantic coast from Virginia to Maine, with a current population of more than thirty-three million; to the north, the Great Lakes-St. Lawrence region is much smaller (about thirteen million) but still growing rapidly. As density of settlement increases in these two areas to the north, south, and east of Vermont, the largely open and undeveloped green area in between assumes a special significance of providing a welcome haven both for active recreation and for rest and repose generally. Vermont is, in effect, the flavor in the sandwich.

In 1985, Vermont began its third consecutive decade of sustained rapid development. After one hundred years of slow change, the economy and landscape of the state are being transformed in a single generation. As a result of the increase in leisure time and the general growth of living standards, many more people have been able to visit areas like Vermont; a considerable number have decided to move and establish residence there. The metropolis has thus been moving in on Vermont.[1]

Moreover, Vermont has not only become more important for those living in the nearby metropolitan areas, it is also far more accessible. Because of the construction of the interstate highway system (see Map 2), much of Vermont now lies within four to five hours of the New York suburbs and within two to three hours of the Boston suburbs, the Hartford-Springfield area, and Montreal.[2] Traffic along the main-traveled corridors in Vermont has increased, and this has been accompanied by a spurt of growth in the same areas, with a variety of recreational, residential, and commercial

11

developments. This combination of growth and new development, along with the inevitable increase in vehicular traffic, has been responsible for many of the recent changes in and threats to the traditional Vermont landscape and townscape. While some growth has occurred throughout the state, the more remote towns have not experienced the degree of change that is rendering substantial parts of the state "minimetropolitan."

INDIGENOUS TRENDS

A series of related changes, primarily occurring locally, have reinforced these trends. The nationwide increase in population and income has resulted locally in more births (for a long period, almost two decades), more activity generally, increased car ownership and more traffic,[3] and various new forms of development. Moreover, the new "in-migrants," usually from nearby metropolitan areas, tend to have a life-style that has reinforced the effects of growth. Some settle in the village centers, but more are scattered across the surrounding countryside in remodeled farmhouses or in new houses. Accustomed to substantial commuting times, the newcomers are likely to regard long trips to work (forty-five minutes or more) as perfectly natural;[4] nor do they question a drive of half the length of the state to attend a meeting or a concert. Moreover, the development of regional shopping centers has sharply increased the practice of shopping in other towns, with consequent damage to the older downtowns. In fact, the principal family shopping may now be done only once a week, especially in families where women are part of the labor force.

Finally, as a consequence of both internal and external factors, recent decades have witnessed a sharp inflation of land prices in many parts of Vermont. At the same time, Vermont agriculture has been in a period of continuing decline with a drastic decrease in the number of working farms. Some of this decrease has been the result of consolidation into larger and more economical units; yet Vermont has experienced an abandonment of agricultural land on a rather large scale,[5] and this naturally has had a marked effect on the landscape—and indirectly on townscape.[6]

A major secondary consequence of the abandonment of agricultural land has been rapid reforestation. The original forest was cleared rapidly after the settlement of Vermont, and from 1830 to 1870—the peak of the sheep-raising era and shortly thereafter—only 25 percent to 30 percent of the state remained in woods. In the early decades of this century, to replant forests on open land was considered a serious civic responsibility. However, by natural ecological processes, northern New England tends to revert to forest as soon as cows and sheep are no longer there to serve as lawn mowers. By 1948, the extent of forest had increased to 57 percent of the state; by 1983, the figure was 76 percent—that is, the proportions were precisely reversed, as compared with the period when a maximum amount of land was cleared a century ago.

12

In this situation, landowners who want to keep an open field free of vegetation for its scenic value have a major job on their hands. The typical Vermont scene has traditionally (at least since the early nineteenth century) included open fields not only along the valley bottom but often extending part way up the hillsides. Yet as the state reverts to forest, relatively few Vermont towns are now surrounded by hills with open fields.[7]

The inflation of land prices has been accompanied by an even more striking inflation in housing cost. As a result, new single-family detached housing—long the ambition of Americans—has become unattainable for many, particularly the young and the elderly. For the first time in generations, a considerable number of service jobs may be available locally for young Vermonters. However, now that they may have the opportunity to live and work in Vermont, the lack of affordable housing has become a major problem, and this may become a brake on the prospects for various economic development proposals. While new "townhouse" developments have a potential for some economies, these also tend to cater to the top of the market. Only one form of housing, the mobile home, is now widely available for the lower-income groups. As a result, mobile homes have multiplied throughout the state, some in mobile-home parks and others scattered around the landscape (or townscape). The state has a mobile-home-park law that provides for the encouragement of such parks, provided that they are screened effectively from adjacent settlements.[8]

THE EXTENT OF GROWTH

Population

The extent of population growth (see Map 3) in the entire state needs to be spelled out as the context for the varying situations in individual towns. After the first settlement by people of European background, the population of Vermont grew rapidly between 1790 and 1830—from about 85,000 to 280,000. The population grew much more slowly as the western migration started, between 1830 and 1870, to a total of 329,000—that is, with an increase of about one thousand persons per year during that period. After 1870, the western migration began in earnest, and the population of the state remained essentially stable for ninety years, expanding by only 60,000 during that long period, i.e., much less than one thousand persons per year. Since 1960, the state's population has been expanding quite rapidly, at a rate of about 60,000 per decade. During the 1960s, about half the population increase came in Chittenden County; during the 1970s, growth spread over most of the state, with only about 25 percent of the increase in Chittenden County.

The recent rapid increase in population has come largely from out-of-state in-migration; as a result, the percentage of the population born out-of-state rose from about 20 percent in 1960 to about 33 percent in 1980. That percentage is much

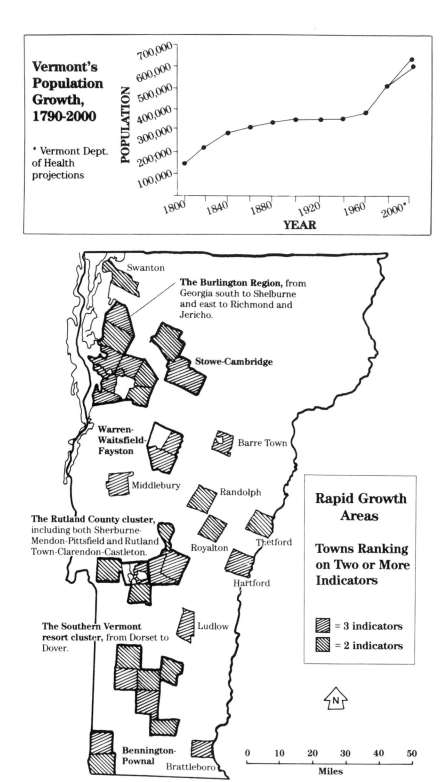

Vermont's Population Growth, 1790-2000

* Vermont Dept. of Health projections

POPULATION / YEAR

The Burlington Region, from Georgia south to Shelburne and east to Richmond and Jericho.

Swanton

Stowe-Cambridge

Warren-Waitsfield-Fayston

Barre Town

Middlebury

Randolph

The Rutland County cluster, including both Sherburne-Mendon-Pittsfield and Rutland Town-Clarendon-Castleton.

Royalton

Thetford

Hartford

Ludlow

The Southern Vermont resort cluster, from Dorset to Dover.

Bennington-Pownal

Brattleboro

Rapid Growth Areas

Towns Ranking on Two or More Indicators

= 3 indicators

= 2 indicators

N

0   10   20   30   40   50
Miles

Map 3.   Rapid Growth Areas

Source: Environmental Law Center, Vermont Law School, Vermont's Next Decade of Growth: Development Policies for the 1980s *(1985), pp. 5, 25.*

higher in the principal resort towns, averaging about 50 percent in Stowe, Manchester, and Woodstock.

Turning to the counties, the statewide pattern indicated above is repeated fairly consistently, except that in this century there has been steady long-term growth in Chittenden County. For example, the population in Franklin County (in the far northwest) was almost exactly the same in 1850 as in 1960, and almost the same is true in Windsor County (in the center). The more rural areas (for example, Orange County) are still well below the 1830 population figures.

The drop in the number of working farms has been dramatic. The population classified as "rural farm" thus has come close to disappearing, with a drop between 1920 and 1980 from about 125,000 to 18,000. Equally striking is the increase of the "rural nonfarm" population from about 118,000 in 1920 (i.e., about the same as the rural farm population) to about 320,000 in 1980—about eighteen times the rural farm population and, in fact, about 60 percent of the population of the entire state.

The long period—almost a century—of near-stable population and little physical development has contributed substantially to the present high quality of townscape in many Vermont towns. In the early nineteenth century, a succession of pleasing and compatible styles dominated Vermont architecture: Federal, Greek Revival, Gothic Revival, and Italianate. The less-attractive architecture characteristic of more recent times has not widely replaced the older buildings.

Employment

The number of jobs in Vermont has been increasing with the same striking rapidity: the labor force in the state increased more than 25 percent in the 1970s. As of the 1980 census, about 25 percent of the total labor force lived in Chittenden County, and about half that number lived in each of three other counties (Rutland, Washington, and Windsor). However, the distribution of the labor force between various levels of skill shows a clear pattern that would be predictable by anyone familiar with the state. On a statewide basis, the number of people in the professional-managerial category increased from 19 percent to 22 percent of the total labor force in the 1970s, while the percentage of those who were classified as operators, fabricators, and laborers dropped by about the same amount, from 18 percent to 16 percent. The overall picture, therefore, is one of considerable expansion of employment with a slight bias toward higher-wage occupations.

The regional distribution is significant. According to 1980 census data, the somewhat-metropolitan counties (Chittenden and Washington) have a larger percentage of employment in the higher-income categories as, for example, professional and managerial work. Conversely, in the more rural areas (the Northeast Kingdom, Grand Isle and Orange counties), the situation is biased more toward the lower-income categories. The agricultural labor force has dropped to about five percent of the total, but is notably higher in the primary agricultural areas in the Champlain Valley (11 percent in both Franklin and Addison) and in some other rural counties, such as Orleans and Orange.

THREATS TO TOWNSCAPE

The most obvious direct effect of rapid growth is the frequent traffic congestion on the highways with all the familiar accompaniments—noise, vibration, air pollution, and serious inconvenience to both visitors and residents. These conditions occur on many highways across the state, particularly at acute seasonal peaks such as during the foliage season (late September and early October), on major ski weekends, and during the late-summer months. As one extreme example, at such times it is not at all unusual to have barely moving bumper-to-bumper traffic from one end of Woodstock village to the other—a phenomenon worthy of New Jersey. Many of the most attractive towns either are remote from traffic or have been effectively bypassed, but traffic problems are pervasive and occasionally acute in several of the larger towns, including Brandon, Chester, Stowe, Woodstock, and perhaps even in Norwich, despite the bypass on the interstate. Heavy traffic through residential areas becomes a serious blight, and those towns that experience such conditions have suffered severely.

One ubiquitous result of increased traffic is the vast increase in the need for parking spaces, both on-street and off-street. Town after town has been dominated not only by traffic but also by parking along its main streets and in blacktop off-street parking lots in the midst of the traditional townscape. Few things can do more harm to the traditional image of a Vermont town, particularly since most parking areas have little or no landscaping. Moreover, there is also an accompanying need for a series of automotive services, which have to go somewhere and which tend to make their presence felt.

THE IMPACT OF NEW DEVELOPMENT

Residential

Quite substantial residential growth has occurred in the developing areas of Vermont. In part, this growth has taken the form of the renovation of deteriorating farmhouses and other structures scattered over the countryside, primarily for use (full-time or part-time) by people from the metropolitan areas. Vermont has also experienced growth in new housing for people retiring to the state (or moving to work there), for seasonal second homes for vacationers, and for others. Some communities (and their surrounding suburban areas) have been growing rapidly, particularly Burlington and Brattleboro. Moreover, near the major ski slopes, quite large developments have taken place, usually in "townhouses" or condominiums, primarily as second homes, at least originally. (These are often processed through zoning mechanisms that are supposed to bring about better design; the supposed improvement is difficult to perceive in the real world.)

As the price of housing has shot up and as taxes have tended to rise along with it, there has been a clear movement toward "gentrification." That is, the traditional economic and social integration of the towns, where everybody has had at least a casual acquaintance with everyone else, has increasingly been superseded by a new and rather homogeneous higher-income population. Many of these newly arrived residents migrated because they wanted to live in places like Vermont. Whether young professionals or retirees, they include a number of energetic activists accustomed to making their weight felt on matters of civic importance. They naturally place great stress on environmental quality; hence local support for scenic protection is now much stronger.

Commercial

Recent changes in commercial land use have been more important and more damaging than residential patterns, particularly in the larger towns. In some of the towns, increased tourist traffic results in drastic changes in the nature of local retailing. Instead of continuing to serve the local population, the commercial area "downstreet" increasingly turns to specialty shops catering primarily to the tourist trade. The existence for a time of several jewelry shops in Stowe and a lollipop shop in Woodstock provides obvious examples. Moreover, there has been substantial growth of very different kinds of home-retailing occupations and of strip commercial development (usually on vacant land along a main road just outside the edge of a village); modern shopping centers, large or small, may pop up anywhere. (They are, of course, "good ratables.")

No more striking examples exist of the downgrading of Vermont's scenic quality than the new commercial strips located at the edge of villages. Here, as elsewhere, highway commercial development and shopping centers undermine the economic base of the traditional downtowns. Moreover, in some instances, ugly new commercial buildings destroy the traditional townscape—usually by replacing older residences— along main roads right in the center of the larger towns (notably in Brandon). Many of the smaller and more remote towns have so far escaped this process, with at most an unobtrusive general store of the "Mom-and-Pop" type. Yet in a few striking instances, new commercial buildings (often garages) blight some of the smaller towns as, for example, on the main corner in Middletown Springs and right in the center of Chelsea.

Discordant fire stations: South Woodstock and Newbury Common

Recreational

Recreational development, one of the main dynamic elements in Vermont, has been concentrated in two types of areas. The most obvious example, and the most important, is the rapid development of new recreation areas with accompanying "villages" adjacent to (or near) the large ski areas—for example, along the Mountain Road in Stowe, along the approaches to the Killington and Sugarbush ski areas, and at Stratton Mountain. As it happens, the major ski areas are usually not immediately adjacent to the most attractive villages,[9] although in many instances, people have moved to such villages (or often visit there) and patronize a ski area not too far away.

Significant recreation-area growth also occurs in areas with water-based recreation, including the Lake Champlain shore, a number of lakes scattered all over, and state parks with water-based recreation.

Community Facilities

Another recent trend has had some negative effect upon Vermont townscape—the occasional tendency toward deconcentration of community facilities in these towns, together with the disintegration or undermining of the traditional activity center. While schools usually have not played a major role in the central concentration of community facilities, they do exist along a number of the commons and have brought a good deal of life to those areas. Yet in several of the towns (as, for example, in Woodstock and Stowe), new high schools have been placed on a rural site outside the town, thus creating a new activity center apart from the traditional one. It also is safe to say that new fire stations usually are incomparably the ugliest buildings anywhere around, followed closely by new post offices.[10]

FUTURE PROSPECTS BY AREAS

Given an understanding of Vermont's role in the Northeast, it is obvious that growth is fairly certain to continue, particularly in certain parts of the state. The most obvious example, Chittenden County, is acting like a normal booming American metropolitan area. The total population is stable in the central city (Burlington), but the suburban population of more than 100,000 is expected to increase by about 50 percent in the next fifteen years.[11] Moreover, substantial growth may be expected to continue in several other areas as, for example, around the major transportation crossroad at White River Junction and generally along the major transportation corridors in the state (see Map 2). Many of the traditional villages are located within such growth areas. Brandon provides a clear example of what is likely to occur with unrestrained growth along Route 7—groups of houses alternate with groups of filling stations and garages.

19

In the smaller, remote villages, the pressure for development is less acute, but recent censuses indicate that growth on a small scale has been occurring in some of these towns. Thus, even in such towns, one should look forward to new residential construction, mostly on vacant land—and so, probably, more on the surrounding hills than in the center—together with some increase in commercial outlets and in community facilities.

Growth inevitably means some loss of traditional character in these towns. At the least, traffic is likely to increase, bringing with it an increased need for parking and probably more commercial facilities often at the ragged edges; further, some of the land around the traditional settlements will be taken up by new buildings. This creeping suburbia has already brought considerable harm to the larger towns; as growth spreads, the more remote ones also are threatened. Moreover, with the decline of Vermont agriculture, the open areas are filling up. In the absence of strong planning guidance and strong enforcement of well-considered zoning and historic district ordinances, irreparable harm will result.

Notes

1. This is part of a larger national trend. From 1945 into the 1970s, American population growth was almost entirely concentrated within metropolitan areas and, more specifically, in the outer parts of such areas. In a striking reversal, more recent studies have shown a considerable shift of growth to rural, nonmetropolitan areas. See *Vermont's Next Decade of Growth: Development Policies for the 1980s.* A Report of the Growth Areas Research Project, Environmental Law Center, Vermont Law School (1985).

2. The 1980 population of the entire New York metropolitan area was 16,121,297; the Boston area, 3,448,122; Montreal, 2,802,485; and Hartford-Springfield, 1,633,437.

3. In 1930, 78,260 automobiles were registered in Vermont; in 1980, the figure was 254,849. The estimated miles of auto travel in the state rose in the same period from 296,800,000 to 3,718,100,000.

4. Native Vermonters (including ex-farmers) are beginning to do the same, sometimes by living on the old farm and driving to a distant job.

5. In 1930, there were 39,006 working farms in Vermont covering 4,639,938 acres. In 1982, there were 6,315 farms with 1,574,441 acres. There are less than 3,000 working dairy farms in Vermont in 1985—down from 30,000 at the turn of the century and 13,000 in 1951.

6. Inflation of land prices has also served to encourage the discontinuance of agriculture by making it more difficult to go into farming and by providing an incentive to shift land into development. See R. Healy and J. Short, *The Market for Rural Land—Trends, Issues, Policies* (1981). See generally R. Brooks and P. Lavigne, "Aesthetic Theory and Landscape Protection: The Many Meanings of Beauty and Their Implications for the Design, Control, and Protection of Vermont's Landscape," 4 UCLA *Journal of Environmental Law and Policy* 128 (1985).

7. There are notable examples in Chelsea, Strafford, and Plymouth. Reforestation of the hillsides is sometimes a relatively recent phenomenon. For example, Blake's Hill overlooking the eastern edge of Woodstock was all open field as recently as 1950; now, the upper half is in thick forest.

8. 10 Vt. Stat. Ann. Sec. 6201 *et seq.*

9. Stowe is the obvious exception. Another striking example is the tiny village of Plymouth, where the center of population is no longer in the traditional area around the Coolidge birthplace; it has shifted to the bottom of the hill in Plymouth Union near the Round Top ski development.

10. The General Services Administration often makes nationwide use of stock standard plans for such facilities. This may (or may not) be an efficient way of saving federal money on architects' fees, but the results are particularly inappropriate in Vermont townscape. Witness the juxtaposition of the shoebox South Royalton post office to the Italianate commercial block and the graceful railroad station.

11. See Vermont Department of Health and Vermont State Planning Office, *Vermont Population Projections 1985-2000* (1983) at 1, prepared after the 1980 census was available. An earlier projection (made before that census) was much higher; see Chittenden County Regional Planning Commission, *We Are Not the Last Generation* (1976), ch. II.

Chapter 2

Characteristics of the Thirty Towns

Numerous common elements recur regularly in many of the towns, but in various combinations, resulting in considerable diversity. Most of these towns are small; a few are noticeably larger but are still towns, not cities (Brandon, Chester, Norwich, Stowe, and Woodstock). Considerable differences exist between the smaller towns and those in this group of larger ones (see Chapter 5). Most of the towns reached their peak of population before the Civil War; only a few are that large now. In the usual pattern, institutional buildings are concentrated around a town common, but again there are exceptions. Most are in the state's middle range in terms of relative wealth; a few are richer, a few poorer.

PRESENT SIZE

Of the thirty communities, the five that are organized politically as separate villages have an average population of less than four hundred. Of the others, about half are settlements located within townships whose total population is less than one thousand. At the other end of the spectrum, the five notably larger towns have township populations ranging from about 2,500 to slightly more than 5,000.

HISTORICAL PATTERN OF GROWTH

In the great majority of these towns, population changes have followed a common pattern: quite rapid growth in the early nineteenth century and massive depopulation (resulting from out-migration from the rural areas) in the late nineteenth and early twentieth centuries, with a definite (but far lesser) revival of growth in recent decades. About half the towns reached their peak population in the censuses of 1830 and 1840; almost all the others did by 1880. Again, about half the towns lost between one-half and two-thirds of their populations between the peak and the twentieth-century low; in six instances (Guildhall, Peacham, Peru, Plymouth, Weston, and Strafford), the loss was about 75 percent.

The extent of recent growth has varied widely. Most of the smaller towns have seen modest increases, in the range of 150 to 250 people; six, mostly much larger, have increased by about one thousand people each. However, the majority remain far below the nineteenth-century peak.[1]

Topography

Most of the towns are located in valley bottoms, usually along a river; the typical site is between two lines of rather dominant hills, one on each side. In a few others, the mountains are on one side only, as with the Green Mountain range east of Brandon.

Three of the towns run along the top of a ridge—Old Bennington, Craftsbury Common, and Randolph Center; five other towns (Grafton, Middletown Springs, Danville, Peacham, and Thetford Hill) have developed by climbing up (or along) a hillside rather than along a relatively flat valley bottom. Except in Danville, nearby hills still dominate the scene.

Most of the towns are located on rivers or brooks, but the streams usually play only a minor role in the local townscape.[2] It is possible in several towns to see where the river flows by, if you look carefully—as in Grafton, Middletown Springs, South Royalton, South Woodstock, and Weston—but the streams are not visually prominent, even there. Only in Woodstock does the river play a significant visual role: the almost-new (1969 and 1974) covered bridge over the Ottauquechee River near the middle of the Green has become perhaps the prime tourist attraction in town (which was precisely its intended purpose). Moreover, the historic Elm Street Bridge has been reconstructed in almost its original form. This was the result of a two-year battle between residents of Woodstock and state highway officials, who wanted to replace it with a "modern concrete bridge."

OPEN FEELING

A striking feature in practically all these towns is the predominant open feeling; most buildings are detached, with plenty of space around them. Only in the larger towns (particularly in Brandon, Woodstock, and, to a lesser extent, South Royalton) is there a substantial group of attached buildings—in each instance, in the downtown commercial area.

INSTITUTIONAL AND COMMERCIAL PATTERNS

The patterns of buildings in the old town centers fall into three categories. In the most frequent situation (with twenty-three examples), the concentration of institutional buildings around the common provides the most familiar image of the attractive New England town. However, both the commons themselves and the institutions around them vary widely.

A second pattern occurs in a few instances with some sort of concentration of institutional buildings, but without a town common. Thus, in Hyde Park, the courthouse and two buildings are located in a large, open space that is not legally the common but is close to the midpoint along the main street. In South Woodstock, an inn and a small store provide a minor focal point of sorts at the north end of town, with the old Academy building not far away.

In a third pattern, a few towns have no concentration of institutional buildings at all, and there is also no common. This is the case in several very small towns (Peru, Plymouth, and Brookfield) and again at the other extreme, along the main street of Stowe.

As for the pattern of commercial development, several towns now have no commercial establishments at all—Old Bennington, Craftsbury Common, and Thetford Hill. Obviously, the residents of these towns do all their shopping elsewhere. Equally obviously, the absence of a commercial building obviates one potential aesthetic blot on the town, and presumably also reduces the amount of local traffic.

Eight towns have a fairly substantial amount of commercial activity. In four of these, the principal commercial area fronts directly on the town common; in the other four, it does not. Of the towns with substantial commercial buildings directly fronting on the common, the most striking example is South Royalton. The entire west frontage of the common consists of a row of Victorian brick buildings, commercial on the ground floor with some residential above, all substantially similar and quite attractive, making this common quite unlike any of the others. Moreover, the south frontage of this common is also unusual: the tracks of the Central Vermont Railroad run all along that frontage, with the old station (now a combination bank and senior citizens' center) in the middle, along with an accessory shed on one side and a modern post office on the other. The other two frontages are more typical, both institutional and residential.

Adjacent commercial facilities (not the prime downtown area) also tend to dominate the relatively small common in Brandon, which is unique in having no residences facing it. The large Brandon Inn is on the east side, with a row of commercial buildings extending along Route 7 to the north; a large supermarket with its parking lots is at the northwest corner; some residences converted into offices are directly to the west; and to the rear (between them and the supermarket), a long, brick building is visible, the national headquarters of the Ayrshire cattle breeders organization. There is a church directly to the north.

Four towns have their principal commercial activity elsewhere, that is, not on the frontage directly across from the common. In Brandon and Woodstock, the principal commercial downtown area just touches one end of the common. In Woodstock, the

Commercial block along the park, South Royalton

The square in Woodstock from the Green

Two fine commercial buildings in Chelsea facing the North Common

town square and shops are directly off the end of the Green, but not on the adjacent frontage; there has been some tendency to convert residences at the near edge of the Green to offices. Much new commercial activity extends east from the center, and more is at the east end of town.

In Norwich, the concentrated commercial area is along the main street directly north of both the common and the point where Route 5 turns sharp right and goes northeast. Norwich, while not having many retail establishments, is unique in having a large number of offices. Finally, Stowe has no common; a substantial number of retail establishments are scattered along the main street (Route 100), along with residences and community facilities, with no particular pattern or focal point. A large number of hotels and similar establishments are located on the Mountain Road going northwest toward Mount Mansfield and Smugglers' Notch.

Sixteen towns (mostly smaller ones) have some relatively minor commercial establishments. In eight towns, these are located opposite the common—in Chelsea, Dorset, East Poultney, Middletown Springs, Newbury, Newfane, Orwell, and Strafford. A distinguished example is in Chelsea, where two handsome old commercial brick buildings are located on the main street directly across from the more northerly of the two commons. There is also a substantial commercial building along one side of the same common.

In most instances, all these establishments are typical "Mom-and-Pop"-type small groceries. The one in Newfane is somewhat larger than that; in Strafford, the only retail establishment is, oddly enough, a bicycle shop serving not just Strafford but a much larger area. In nine others, the minor commercial establishments are located apart from a common, usually because no common exists. In Grafton, the store is down the road from the common, which is located in an unusual spot off-center at the uphill end of town; in Montgomery, the store is just off the common. In Randolph Center, a similar shop plus a post office are located near the middle of town with the community institutions at the south end. Peacham has a somewhat similar situation.

THE COMMON

In the typical pattern, the village common is an integral (and important) part of the central complex in a relatively small town. This is the situation in Craftsbury Common, Danville, East Poultney, Guildhall, Montgomery, Newbury, Newfane, Old Bennington, Orwell, South Royalton, Strafford and Weston. In the larger towns, the situation is somewhat different: the central business district is often larger and more concentrated, with the village common located immediately adjacent to it, as in Woodstock and Brandon. In Chelsea and Norwich, the shopping facilities are more limited, but the com-

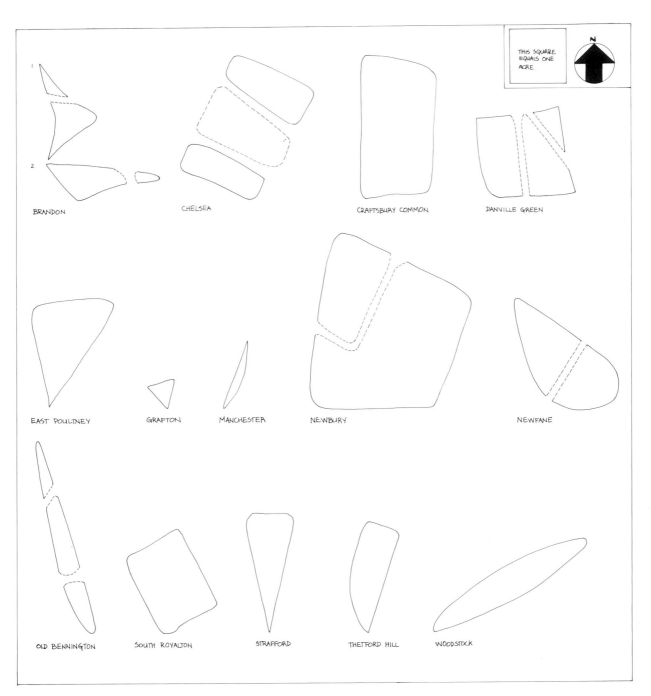

THIS SQUARE EQUALS ONE ACRE

N

BRANDON

CHELSEA

CRAFTSBURY COMMON

DANVILLE GREEN

EAST POULTNEY

GRAFTON

MANCHESTER

NEWBURY

NEWFANE

OLD BENNINGTON

SOUTH ROYALTON

STRAFFORD

THETFORD HILL

WOODSTOCK

Diagrams show the size and shape of many of the commons involved in this study, all at the same scale

mons are similarly situated. In a few instances, the common is located in another visually prominent position at the upper end of the main street, as in Grafton and Strafford, and at the lower end in Thetford Hill.

Size

The commons vary widely in size. In a couple of instances, they are strikingly large—about seven-and-one-half acres in Newbury and about three acres in Craftsbury Common. At the other extreme, some of them are tiny: in Chester, Dorset, and Manchester, the common is merely a small strip along the main street, barely noticeable visually and performing no function beyond a minor aesthetic one. In Grafton, the common is visually important at the uphill end of the main street, next to one church and near another, but it is still only a small triangle. In most of the other towns with a common, the common is of medium size (approximately one acre).

Shape

The commons also show several patterns as to shape. Quite a few are rectangular, as are those in Craftsbury Common and South Royalton, and both commons in Chelsea (and probably originally in Danville and Newbury). About an equal number are triangular in shape, as in East Poultney, Grafton, Strafford, and Thetford Hill. The common in Newfane is more or less pear-shaped, bisected by the main road. A striking variation appears in Woodstock: the Green is long and narrow in the shape of a large ocean liner; local rumor has it that this was based on the exact size and shape of the nineteenth-century ocean liner "Great Eastern."

Relative Wealth

Analysis of the relative wealth in the various towns in 1980—specifically, of the median family income[3]—provides a clear pattern. Speaking generally, seven of the ten wealthiest towns in the state (measured this way) are suburbs of Burlington; this obviously reflects the large influx into those towns of professional-level people working at new centers of high-wage employment there. Again speaking generally, the great majority of the towns in the state are lumped together within a not particularly broad range. Of 246 populated towns for which figures are reported, 175 are bunched fairly close together in the range between $13,000 and $18,000; most of the thirty towns analyzed here are in this group. In the state as a whole, thirty towns reported median family incomes of $19,000 or above; one hundred six more are in the range of $15,000 to $18,000; and sixty-nine are in the range of $13,000 to $15,000. Only twenty-two towns were below the $13,000 level.

Turning first to the figures on the townships involved in the present study (see Table 1), Norwich is by far the wealthiest (and stands third in the state) with a median

TABLE 1
MEDIAN FAMILY INCOME: VERMONT TOWNS

Rank Among Thirty Towns	Rank in State	Town	Income
1	3	Norwich	$25,313
2	16	Dorset	20,559
3	25	Peru	19,271
4	43	Woodstock	18,133*
5	50	Manchester	17,878
6	52	Newfane	17,841
7	53	Stowe	17,833
8	59	Chester	17,500
9	72	Danville	17,222
10	76	East Poultney	17,049
11	78	Guildhall	17,000
12	90	Middletown Springs	16,696
13	103	Bennington	16,452**
14	105	Thetford Hill	16,418
15	107	Grafton	16,324
16	122	Brookfield	15,917
17	126	Weston	15,809
18	136	Hyde Park	15,496
19	144	Plymouth	15,234
20	145	Randolph Center	15,234
21	152	Orwell	15,000
22	166	Strafford	14,762
23	180	Brandon	14,355
24	187	South Royalton	14,037
25	192	Newbury	13,877
26	195	Peacham	13,854
27	196	Craftsbury Common	13,846
28	198	Chelsea	13,750
29	236	Montgomery	11,845

* Includes South Woodstock.
** Really irrelevant—this is for the whole city.

family income of $25,313, followed at a substantial distance by Dorset with $20,559 and Peru (surprisingly) with $19,271. These two rank sixteenth and twenty-fifth in the state, respectively. Much lower, at number forty-three, is Woodstock with $18,133, clearly reflecting the town's large lower-middle income service population, which is apparently missing in the wealthier towns. At the other end of the spectrum, Montgomery is near the very bottom with a median income of $11,845; Newbury, Craftsbury, and Chelsea are in the range between $13,000 and $14,000.

Figures on 1980 median family income are available for the villages (see Table 2), and these modify the picture somewhat. Old Bennington comes out at the very top, well ahead of Norwich. Woodstock village ranks slightly higher than Woodstock town, and South Woodstock probably would, too (depending on how it is defined). Manchester village is much higher, ranking between Norwich and Dorset among the thirty towns.

TABLE 2
MEDIAN FAMILY INCOME: VERMONT VILLAGES

Village	Income
Old Bennington	$30,528
Manchester	23,438
Woodstock	18,641
Hyde Park	16,667
Stowe	16,904
Newbury	14,688
Newfane	14,167

Notes

1. In five instances, the pattern of growth at least *looks* rather different (Bennington, Manchester, Poultney, Brandon, and Randolph), but the difference derives more from the nature of the information available than from a variation in the growth pattern. In these towns, the only information available over the long period—the total for the entire township—shows fairly consistent growth over the whole period; but, except in Brandon, the townscape with which we are concerned is not in the township's principal settlement. For this secondary settlement and its pattern of growth, no separate figures are available over the entire long period; they probably followed the prevailing pattern elsewhere.

The statistical problem arises from the fact that the census has normally reported figures for each separate governmental unit only. Since only a few of our towns are organized separately as villages, in most instances there are no population figures to distinguish a secondary settlement from the others within a township or, for that matter, from the rural population generally. In the few instances of a separately organized "village," these have usually been organized as such only recently, so that no historical sequence in depth is available. The analysis above has therefore been done in terms of townships. Since the results are so clear-cut and repetitive, this gives a generally accurate picture.

Most of the mid-nineteenth and late-nineteenth-century out-migration was from rural areas, and so there are often abandoned settlements scattered all over such areas. The older central parts of the towns have not been affected as much; most of the buildings there are old and remain intact. However, it is true that some commercial and particularly some industrial establishments have disappeared, occasionally leaving noticeable gaps or groups of cellar holes.

The concentration herein, therefore, is on what are really villages; about half of these are secondary settlements within a township.

2. Most Vermont towns have been built with their backs to the local river, so to speak. For a strong plea to turn them around and give the citizens a chance to enjoy the river, see Bennington County Regional Planning Commission, *The Vermont River: Heritage and Promise* (1975).

3. Statisticians generally regard the figure on median family income as the most reliable index of the wealth of a town. Figures on average family income can be biased by a substantial number of people at the bottom of the range or by a very few at the top. This problem does not occur to the same extent with the figures on median income.

The Newfane Inn from the common

Chapter 3

Historical Development and the Commons

The town common is one of the most familiar features of a New England town and provides one of its prime amenities. The village commons in these towns vary widely as to location, size, shape, ownership, and function. In most instances, the common plays a significant role in the life and appearance of the towns. But in spite of their importance, scholarly information is not widely available, and often the history of particular commons is unknown even to local inhabitants and officials.[1] Most New England commons, along with their accompanying early uses and legal attributes, share a "common" history with, and derive from, the commons in the English and Welsh towns from which most of the early settlers emigrated.

According to John Stilgoe (see Note 1), much of the character of New England common lands derives from ancient English land use laws. English common law recognized two types of land: one belonged to private individuals, the other to the monarchy. The royal land was, in practice, unowned land and served the general public, which had certain less-than-fee rights therein. These legal rights to the unowned land were usually divided by use. Stilgoe mentions that under English common law, the right to graze livestock or a "common of pasture" existed on the royal land. There was also a "common of estovers" or right to cut wood for building or fuel (but not for sale); a "common of turbary" or right to dig peat; a "common of piscary" or right to take fish in freshwater; and a "common in the soil" or right to take sand and stone. Unfortunately, it was usually only the private landowners or "householders" who held these rights to use the commons. The landless poor, known as cottagers, were rarely eligible for such rights.

During the sixteenth century, rising prices and population brought great pressure upon the royal land. Nobles petitioned the King to allow the commons to be used for more profitable uses, such as sheep grazing. The householders objected, but the King began reassigning the land. Many householders lost their privileges to use the common land as it was assigned to other uses, and the distinctions between householders and cottagers began to erode. The colonial English settlers in New England had, for the most part, been disgruntled householders, though some were cottagers aspiring to a new social position. According to Stilgoe, the settlers' memories of their rights to the common, coupled with the community-based nature of Puritanism, led to the adoption of strong common land systems in early New England. The Puritans used the common land system, in part, to enforce religious conformity: members of the community who did not conform lost their rights to use the common land.

Early commons in New England developed in several different ways, and each method influenced the eventual development of commons in Vermont. Each community created its own common land system. The rights to these new commons were, at first, used in traditional ways. Each farmer, on the way to the fields, left his cows in a central "close" where livestock was penned before and after grazing on outlying common pasture. The cows were driven from the close to the common pasture on the outskirts of town. The central "close" often became the town common, as did the pasture in other places. The extent of community common land and the legal rights of estovers, piscary, etc., depended in large part on the geography contained by the town boundaries. Some coastal communities in Massachusetts still auction fishing rights to common fishing grounds at their annual town meetings. Remnants of the common land system still exist in many New England towns, holding on in the form of town forests or town beaches.

The idea of a common pasture lasted for centuries. In many coastal towns, the pasture was often a small island used for the entire summer. In New Hampshire, for generations the mountainsides were common pastures. Elected land assignment committees often apportioned the common pasture among the "first-comers and their descendants." Some towns assigned to larger house lots larger rights to the common land, while others based rights to common land on family size.

Problems with use of the commons grew with questions of transfer of rights and with inmigration into the towns. If newcomers came to town, did they acquire a right to pasture on the already overcrowded common? What rights in common did the descendants of first-comers enjoy? Were such rights to be equally apportioned between son and daughter? These questions created much confusion in debates in many towns. The more populous newcomers often succeeded at terminating the common pasture system via the town meeting. (It may have been here that the native-versus-flatlander debate first started!) The land assignment committees sold extra shares of the common pasture to pay for schools and public buildings. Gradually, most towns sold or otherwise disposed of all useful outlying common pasture land.

Even as this traditional system of agricultural use was dying, a parallel system increased in importance. The early Puritans avoided the word "church," preferring to speak of "congregation" and referring to the church building as the meetinghouse. Early town planners felt the meetinghouse should stand at the center of town on a special piece of land called the meetinghouse "lot." This "lot" was often large and used for a variety of purposes. It may have served as the close, the burying ground, and the militia training ground. The portion most often used for secular activities was sometimes separated from the lot and called the town common. As the Congregational Church's hold on town government began to slip, many of the congregations surrendered their quasi-ownership of the common to the town.

In most Vermont towns, settled more than 150 years later than those in southern New England, the later trends were more important. Many who migrated northward into the wilderness of the "New Hampshire Grants" chose to settle on dispersed farmsteads in their new towns and did not depend on the common pasture system. (Of the towns profiled here, only Randolph Center seems to have gone through the entire cycle of close to common to disposal.) They did carry with them, however, the familiar pattern of meetinghouse and common and used this idealized form for the layout of many villages.

The development of the commons played a central role in the development of these towns. Investigation of individual town histories, however, illuminates the many different paths of development of both the commons and the towns as a whole. Historical profiles of Chelsea, Newbury, Randolph Center, and Strafford illustrate both the difficult question of what in the current townscape is historically accurate and what is essential in the preservation of valued townscape features.

CHELSEA

Chartered in 1781, Chelsea is unique among Vermont villages in that it has two town commons in close proximity, separated by a row of buildings and a stream. The North Common grew out of a town vote in 1791 to buy two acres for a common. After the original negotiations were unfruitful, another committee in 1794 began negotiations with a changed purpose, seeking "a piece of land for a public parade."[2] A local militia captain became interested in the proposition, and in 1795, he deeded the North Common land to the town for the sum of five pounds.

The South Common is connected with Chelsea's status as a shire town or county seat. The first county courthouse was built in 1796 along Chelsea's main road. The courthouse soon proved inadequate, and in 1802, land was deeded to the town for a courthouse and jail and additional land for a "new common." One stipulation in the deed specified the land must be leveled and cleared of stones. In 1810, a new courthouse opened, situated at the head of the new South Common. In 1811, the town was given an option to buy the land between the two commons for the use of a common and a parade ground, but it expired unused in 1821. In 1829, the land was divided and built upon. However, in the intervening years, this land had been cleared, and it seems that the two commons were temporarily one, divided only by the brook that runs between them.

The early history of the South Common reflected its connection with the justice system. It is believed that stocks and a whipping post were constructed on this com-

The courthouse and the South Common in Chelsea. Parking is making inroads into the common.

mon at one time, and it was also the site of one of the village's more gruesome incidents. In 1836, a gallows was set up with the intention of executing convicted murderer Rebecca Peake. Peake spared the town the spectacle, however, by poisoning herself in her jail cell the night before. The present courthouse replaced the earlier one on the same site in 1847 with jail cells (now unused) in the back.

Presently, neither common has any monuments. A small, new bandstand was built and given to the town on the North Common in 1983 by a Hollywood studio, which filmed part of a movie in Chelsea and had needed the bandstand for a prop. The town removed the bandstand in 1985 because of vandalism and the expense of maintenance.

NEWBURY

The Newbury common, one of the largest and most actively used in Vermont, is of relatively recent origin. The town, however, is one of the oldest in Vermont. Settled on heights overlooking the Connecticut River, it was in 1763 one of the first Vermont towns granted a charter by New Hampshire Governor Benning Wentworth. The town proprietors also later acquired a New York charter that, echoing the political dispute of the time, refers to the "pretended New Hampshire charter."

Neither the New York nor the New Hampshire charter contains any provisions relating to a common, and the village had none until part of the land that constitutes the present common was given to the Methodist Society in 1829 for the construction of a church.[3] This building still stands: the church and the part of the common upon which it stands are now owned by the Newbury Women's Club.

The central factor in the growth of the town common was, however, a decision made by a session of the New Hampshire Conference of the Methodist Episcopal Church. Meeting at Northfield, New Hampshire, in 1833, a conference committee announced Newbury had been selected as the site for a new seminary because of its central location between New Hampshire and New York plus a positive reaction by the town. In response to overtures by the committee, the town had pledged $6,000 (to be matched by the conference) on the condition that the seminary be located there. In 1833, the original seminary building was erected next to the church on a large tract of land (which included nearly all the present common) purchased with the matching funds. Later that year, after the seminary received its Vermont charter, the town bought an adjacent residence, removed the buildings, and added the land to the portion of the seminary farm that had been set apart for a common. At the same time, the town spent $700 filling a large gully originally caused by a severe storm in 1795; thus, the bounds of the common were set about as they are now.

The seminary remained in Newbury until 1867, when it was removed to Montpelier as the result of some local maneuverings that were apparently "not credit-

39

able to the honesty or sagacity of those who conspired to bring about the removal."[4] In 1887, the original seminary building and the common were deeded to Newbury School District No. 4, and the building was occupied by the village grade school. The old building was razed shortly after 1900, and the new grade school on the site is still used today.

The original layout of the common has changed somewhat with a new road passing in front of the school building and church, and the corners have been rounded to accommodate automobiles. The seven-and-one-half acres of common include separate softball and Little League fields, several plaques, a flagpole, tree-lined walkways, and a grassy knoll topped by a flower bed.

RANDOLPH CENTER

First settled in 1778 by a frontiersman from Hanover, New Hampshire, Randolph Center was, until 1891, the religious, educational, and social center of the area that now encompasses the town and village of Randolph. Unlike Chelsea and Newbury, the concept of land held for the "common" good was integral to Randolph Center from the start. The original town charter, executed by the governor, council, and general assembly in 1781, set aside:

> . . . 5 equal shares or rights to be appropriated to the public uses following, vis, one share or right for the use of a seminary or college within the state; one share or right for the use of the county grammar school throughout this state; one share or right for the first settled minister of the gospel in said Township, to be disposed of for that purpose, as the inhabitants thereof shall direct; one share or right for the support of the ministry; one share or right for the benefit and support of the school or schools within said Township.

The several purposes of these shares of land appropriated to common public use were met, for the most part, within the small area now known as Randolph Center. The first meetinghouse was a log structure built in 1784 on Sunset Hill "as near as possible" to the geographical center of the township. Where the trail running north and south crossed the one running east and west, about where the present elementary schoolhouse is located, the town laid out a cemetery and, just north of it, a three-acre common.[5] In 1791, a new meetinghouse was begun on the east border of the common, and the town meeting in March voted to move "the Stocks and Sign Post" to the meetinghouse.

Because of the town's location in the geographical center of the state, the settlers hoped it would be named the state capital. In anticipation, the main street right-of-way was laid out ten rods (165 feet) wide. Main Street is now off center in this right-of-way, and the right-of-way overlaps portions of the original common. In 1791, the main road was below the elementary school, and the South Randolph Road crossed alongside the cemetery. From 1791 until 1837, the meetinghouse served both as the meeting place for town affairs and as the church for the Congregational Society. In 1837, the meetinghouse was sold to the society, and the town secured meeting rights to the basement of the new Church of Equal Rights, which was built across the way.

In 1795, fifteen to twenty horse sheds were built on the common near the meetinghouse; they served to shelter farm horses until automobiles entered Randolph. Like the pews of the meetinghouse, the sheds were private property frequently transferred by deed as real estate, although the land was never deeded to the owners. Until a few years before the Civil War, the common occasionally saw use as a parade ground to drill the local militia (able-bodied males from 16 to 20) under their elected officers. Other uses included grazing of the horses, a playground, and a public place of punishment.

In 1880, the Church of Equal Rights burned and was rebuilt in the next year as the present Methodist Church building. A new town hall was built on the common where the schoolhouse now stands. The town hall burned in 1893; two years after, town meetings and, therefore, the social and business focus of the town, shifted to (West) Randolph. The major portion of the population and the only real business district remain there to this day.

The present elementary school was built in 1903; physical layout and use of the common have changed little since then. Bisected diagonally by the road, the common now consists of one small triangle behind the schoolhouse, bordering the cemetery, and a larger triangle behind the Congregational Church. Because of the original grant in the town charter for the use of "a seminary or college," the areas immediately north and east of the common have, over the years, served as sites for a succession of educational institutions: the Academy in 1804; Randolph State Normal School in 1867; State Agricultural School in 1911; and, in 1957, the Vermont Technical Institute, which has evolved into the present two-year Vermont Technical College. The college campus now extends from the north and east sides of the common north to the intersection of Main Street and Route 66.

The triangle behind the schoolhouse is used as a playground and is fenced in to keep the children from wandering. Until recently, twenty-seven maples lined the edge of the road from the schoolhouse nearly to the end of the cemetery. They were removed partly because of damage from road salt, although the stumps are still visible. The triangle behind the church serves as a playground for the older school children. It borders, on two sides, the campus of Vermont Technical College and also lacks several border trees. The major, and perhaps only, summertime use of this section is for softball games by students and community residents. The common receives almost no maintenance and resembles a hay pasture gone to seed. It is cut once or twice yearly by a local farmer, the cuttings left on the ground to rot.

A strip of open, grassy "common area" created by the wide Main Street right-of-way starts from the Congregational Church and runs north along the college campus. A similar, narrower strip borders the private homes on the opposite side of the street. A section next to the church is maintained by the college as a community skating rink in the winter, so green benches line the edges.

Use and maintenance of the rest of the common area have been points of dispute between citizens and the college at times. In the mid 1960s, the college decided to build a "stone wall" along the front section of the campus on Main Street. Citizen outrage arose after approximately three hundred feet of the "stone wall" went up. The "stones" were waste slabs from the granite quarry hauled in by large trucks and set in place with cranes. Because the wall was within the Main Street right-of-way, the town prevailed upon the college to remove the wall before it was completed.

STRAFFORD

Strafford was chartered by New Hampshire Governor Benning Wentworth in 1761 to a group of proprietors who met and organized in Hebron, Connecticut. The first settlement was established in 1768, but it was not in the upper village area where the common is located. As Gwenda Smith, town historian, notes:

> While it seems only natural to find a village here at this intersection of major local roads, the name "Old City" serves to remind us that this was not the place chosen by the earliest settlers. When the Town House was built a generation or so later, however, it was located closer to the geographical center of the town. . . . A village soon grew around the Town House and whatever other early buildings may have stood near it. A dam across the brook powered a mill or two, and close by was an already flourishing general store and tavern. They would all be given a boost in 1809 when the route of the Norwich to Chelsea turnpike was laid out through the village.[6]

The Town House was built in 1799 on the hill overlooking the present common. Its outward appearance has changed little over the years. The common, deeded to the town in 1802, has seen many changes in the intervening years. The roads crisscrossed it in the first one hundred years; buildings and trees have come and gone. Apparently, the land comprising the common was somewhat swampy, for in 1906 the Village Improvement Society spent some time filling and shaping the common into its current form. Ironically, given its history, the Strafford common is one of the most picturesque and well-known throughout the world due to its many appearances in *National Geographic, Vermont Life*, the CBS "World News" and Charles Kuralt's "On the Road" television series. The common and Town House area are maintained by the town, and both are included in the 120-acre Strafford Village National Register Historic District.

The majestic Town House is still used for town meetings and an occasional wedding or Easter Sunday service. The common hosts the annual PTA Fourth of July fair and parade accompanied by a fire department barbecue. The firefighters also sponsor a lobster bake on the common each August.

Notes

1. The major works focusing on town commons include a helpful unpublished master's thesis entitled *The Village Green Ensemble in Northern Vermont* by John Biddle Meyer (University of Vermont, 1974). *On Common Ground* by Ronald Lee Fleming and Lauri A. Halderman (Harvard Common Press, 1982) is equally helpful, particularly the chapter by John Stilgoe, "Town Common and Village Green in New England: 1620–1981," *On Common Ground* at 7. Other useful general sources include Abby M. Hemenway's *The Historical Gazetteer of Vermont* and *Potash and Pine—The Formative Years in Vermont History* by Leigh Wright (Greenhills Press, 1977).

2. Comstock, John M., *Chelsea, Vermont* (1955) at 15. "A parade" refers not to the modern pageant but to a military training ground upon which the militia would drill or "parade."

3. Wells, Frederic P., *History of Newbury, Vermont from the Discovery of Coos County to the Present Time* at 183.

4. *Ibid.*

5. Cooley, Harry H., *Randolph Vermont Historical Sketches*, Greenhills Press (1978) at 15.

6. Historical Notes—1981 Strafford Town Report.

Chapter 4

The Prime Elements of Amenity in Vermont Towns

A detailed analysis of the thirty Vermont towns makes it clear that certain common and generally pleasing elements recur regularly and play a dominant role in the appearance of these towns. No one town has all of these elements, but all of these towns have several of them—and most have most of them. Moreover, these common elements occur in different combinations in different towns, resulting in considerable diversity. These elements may be summarized briefly as follows.

MAJOR FACTORS

A Rural Setting

A concentrated settlement is dominated by the rural setting, usually involving a mountain backdrop, and often emphasized by the fields extending directly behind the houses that extend along the single street.

A Focal Point

A central focal point, which stands in people's minds as the prime image of the community, gives the town a sense of identity. This physical focal point—often accentuated by good urban design—may be, and often is, also the center of major community activities. It may be the local common, some major institutional buildings (a church or a courthouse), or some commercial development. The common is almost always centrally located and may vary widely in size, shape, and function.

Human Scale

Both the buildings and the adjacent open spaces in the central area are consistently at the human scale, i.e., 1½-stories to 2½-stories high. Moreover, few buildings are longer than the average house, and the front and side yards are in proportion.

Architectural Quality

Architectural quality is consistently high in the central area, with few strikingly incompatible buildings.

SECONDARY CHARACTERISTICS

A second group of characteristics, while not present universally, occur in quite a few of the towns. These include no heavy through traffic, only small-scale commercial facilities, landscaping that is often impressive, a sense of complete enclosure around the common, and a notable lack of clutter.

THE RURAL CONTEXT

Views of the Surrounding Mountains

In almost all instances, the towns are surrounded by superb views. In the great majority of cases (twenty-three), the towns are located on the valley bottom—often on a small plateau just above the river level, avoiding the flood plain—and are dominated by large and very visible hills.[1] This is, of course, simply a reflection of the fact that Vermont is a mountainous state. The main ridge of the Green Mountains runs north and south up the center of the state (actually, slightly west of the center), but there are substantial hills covering most of the state, except in the Champlain Valley in the northwest and in Essex County in the Northeast Kingdom. Only in a few instances have the larger towns started to climb up the hillside, notably in Woodstock, Norwich, and Stowe.

The significance of these constant hillside views is underlined by the nature of Vermont scenery. A distinctive feature of the Vermont rural scene, particularly in contrast to New Hampshire, is that the open fields along the valley bottom often extend up the adjacent hillside. (In Vermont, there are relatively few spectacular scenes—only an occasional vista of the major mountains opening up suddenly in the middle-to-far distance.) The characteristic Vermont rural scene is a view from ridgetop to ridgetop, with open meadowlands along the stream in the valley bottom, occasionally marked with stone walls and with buildings, and with infinitely varying patterns of open fields and forest along the slope of the hillside. While, in most cases, the hillsides are wooded by now, this pattern is evident from Chelsea, South Woodstock, and Plymouth, and, to some extent, in Brookfield, Craftsbury Common, Strafford, and Thetford Hill.

The types of hillside views visible from these Vermont towns vary considerably. The most common pattern is for the hills to extend along two sides of a valley with the town along a river at the valley bottom, though there are some exceptions. A few towns are, in effect, located in a bowl, with hills at roughly the same scale (and distance) extending all around, as in Plymouth and Weston. (Similarly, Orwell occupies its own small bowl.)[2] Occasionally, the view is more impressive with large mountains

The North Common and the open slopes to the west, Chelsea

The North Common, the church, and wooded hillsides to the east, Chelsea

The square and Mt. Tom, Woodstock

The courthouse, the library, and Mt. Peg, Woodstock. Wooded hilltops are visible from all Woodstock streets.

The Congregational Church and Mt. Tom, Woodstock

The White River and South Royalton from the north

KEVIN EATON

The main range of the central Green Mountains (Killington and Pico) as seen from the ridgetop town of Randolph Center

Manchester dominated by Mount Equinox

Old Bennington and the mountains to the southwest

The commercial district along Main Street in Stowe, facing east

The commercial district along Main Street in Stowe, facing west

nearby, notably in Newbury (looking across the river into New Hampshire), and also in Manchester and Old Bennington. Another striking phenomenon is the existence of hills enclosing the view at one end of the main street or at both ends: this is a principal amenity in Stowe and is also quite evident in Dorset and South Woodstock.

The ridgetop towns have striking vistas that are very different from the usual pattern. Old Bennington is, of course, part of Bennington, although sharply separated topographically and strikingly different. The village of Old Bennington (incorporated as a separate municipality) runs north and south along the top of a ridge at the western edge of Bennington. The town common, although unhappily often dominated by heavy traffic, provides a strong focal point for the village; there is a superb church along with many attractive houses, huge trees, and fine views of quite large, distant mountains. The Battle Monument is located on a cul-de-sac at the north end of the village. Craftsbury Common, by contrast, is a small, isolated settlement running along the bare top of a broad ridge surrounded by flat open fields; there are some considerable views of the mountains across the adjoining valleys.

One Street Wide

The rural context of Vermont townscape is strongly reinforced by another phenomenon that is widespread in these towns. With exceptions only in the larger towns (Brandon, Chester, Norwich, Stowe, and Woodstock), these towns are essentially only one street wide—often widening briefly at the common. In other words, houses (and other buildings) are located along both sides of a single main street; behind each house, and visible between the houses at frequent intervals, one can see the characteristic Vermont pattern, with open fields leading up to a forest edge and with forests usually covering the upper hillside. This pattern is most apparent in Thetford Hill, where there is a fairly wide spacing of buildings on the uphill side of the main street; looking between the buildings, one sees meadows perhaps two hundred yards deep leading up to the forest edge. Other examples are found in Brookfield, Manchester, Newfane, Strafford, and Weston.

A particularly striking example of this pattern (and its value) occurs along the Mountain Road (Route 108) running north from the center of Stowe toward Smuggler's Notch. For about five miles, a constant succession of motels and other tourist-oriented commercial establishments are usually set amid large lawns. The total effect is quite pleasant compared to the usual commercial strip development. On the other hand, if parallel streets lined with buildings extended along either side, so that the views between buildings extended just to the rear ends of other buildings, the result would be completely different. Since there are no such streets, in almost all instances one looks past the motels and other buildings to the usual Vermont pattern of open fields and forest, with no sense of being in a crowded town.

57

View between buildings to the fields behind and the forest edge, next to the former library in Thetford Hill

View past buildings to the fields behind and the forest edge, taken from the Town House in Strafford

South Royalton: the view from near I-89 to the south. The park (common) dominates the town center and provides the focal point.

While the pattern described above is dominant, the towns exhibit a number of minor variations. In particular, the settlement often widens to two blocks (or a bit more) at the town common. This is apparent in about one-third of the towns—most obviously in Newfane, but also in Chelsea, Craftsbury Common, Danville, East Poultney, Newbury, Orwell, South Royalton, and Weston.[3]

Open Feeling

These towns are more like villages than cities; and so in overall impression, the townscape is dominated by an open feeling. Specifically, in all the towns, the buildings are predominantly detached, often with substantial side yards, except that in some of the larger towns there may be a group of attached buildings at the commercial center (as in Brandon and Woodstock).

Open Space Coming Right Into Town

Another feature strongly reinforces the rural feeling in about half these towns: a piece of the open countryside comes into town, right up to the main street.[4] In a number of towns, a vacant lot on the main street is visually part of the continuous open country stretching out behind. In some instances, this is a pleasant addition to the rural atmosphere, as in Plymouth and in South Woodstock along the whole southern half of the village. In the latter instance, the east side of the main street is part of the open country behind. In a few others (as in East Poultney and South Royalton), such open space serves to interrupt the sense of enclosure and may be a minus factor.

THE TOWN CENTER—A CENTRAL FOCAL POINT

As John Reps has pointed out, city planning did not simply start in this century; many of the older American towns show unmistakable signs that at least certain elements were planned carefully,[5] along with other indications that they "just growed." It is, therefore, probably not accidental that the layout of these towns often provides a natural physical focal point in the center.[6] Such a focal point can play several important roles. It provides a sense of community identity; this is what residents think of when they think of "our town." ("There is a there, there.")[7] Moreover, it provides a central point for community interaction and is often a site for major community activities. The focal point is usually at the common, if there is one, or more often at the common plus the associated institutional or commercial buildings.[8] Where there is no green, the focal point may be in an institutional grouping (as in Hyde Park)[9] or at the local store on the main corner (as in Norwich, Peru, and Plymouth). Or there may be no focal point at all, as in Stowe, Brookfield, and Randolph Center.

Newfane common and the courthouse complex

The church right on the common, East Poultney

THE SURROUNDINGS OF THE COMMON

Institutional Buildings Around a Town Common

Another major amenity in these towns is one of their most familiar features—a concentration of major institutional buildings at one point, normally together with some residences and minor commercial development, and usually around the town common. Twenty-three towns have commons, and in all (except Grafton and Randolph Center), the common is at a central point with some institutions around. Two others, in Hyde Park and South Woodstock, have a similar concentration but at a spot that is not a town common. In a few instances, major buildings are located within the boundaries of the common. The most striking examples are found in the courthouse complex in Newfane and the church in East Poultney.

In the twenty-three towns with commons, the most typical public buildings, and historically the most important surrounding the common, are the church[10] (often Congregational with white clapboard and a white spire) and the inn,[11] usually descended from an ancient tavern. Residences are almost invariably present (except in Brandon), and other public buildings occur on the common in most instances. The precise figures for the number of towns with one or more examples of each of the above are as follows:[12]

Residence	22
Church	21
Inn	11
Minor Commercial	10
School	9
Library	8
Post Office	7
Town Hall	7
Courthouse	5

While the figures on relative frequency are interesting, they do not show the relative importance of the various buildings. The important public function of certain institutional buildings—particularly courthouses and churches—is reflected in the increased size of their buildings and their commanding dignity. In the five county seats (Chelsea, Guildhall, Manchester, Newfane, and Woodstock), the large courthouse naturally plays an important role visually and in the life of the town. The frequency of churches and inns tells us a lot about New England history, and these usually stand out in this area.

Residences are almost always present, and this tends to soften the impact of the larger institutional buildings. The library is likely to be an important building, both

The grade school, former church, and part of the common in Newbury

JOAN LIGHTFOOT

Craftsbury Common facing the academy. Here the common is used as a playing field.

The Church and the common, Old Bennington

The Town House, Strafford, from the common

The church and the courthouse at the uphill ends of the two commons in Chelsea

TOM HOBAN

The church and courthouse together with the Equinox House across the street form a central focal point in Manchester.
Note the small remnant of the common in the middle of the street.

TOM HOBAN

architecturally and in terms of its use. The schools do not play as important a role visually as one might expect; the same is usually true of the town hall (or town offices). The minor commercial establishments are usually unobtrusive; the post office (and, occasionally, a fire station) often strikes a discordant note.

The town common and the related institutions normally provide the visual focal point of the town and usually are the activity centers as well. In quite a number of instances, the institutional buildings (and also the residences) include some fine buildings; in fact, some of the finest architecture in the state occurs at these locations. Obvious examples include the churches at Old Bennington and East Poultney, the former church on the hill (now the Town House) beyond the common in Strafford, the courthouse complex in Newfane, the courthouses in Chelsea and Woodstock, and the Equinox House in Manchester.

The Human Scale

Another factor is equally important. With few exceptions (the principal instances, in public buildings, are noted above), the buildings in the central part of these towns are at a small and quite human scale. The buildings fronting on the common are usually 1½-stories to 2½-stories high, almost invariably with a gable; normally, only the church spire (or tower) and the courthouse are taller. Moreover, with few exceptions, no buildings have front walls much longer than those of a good-sized house. Obviously, any tall building placed here would change the appearance completely, and the few examples of long buildings have a somewhat similar effect.

Apart from the churches and courthouses, the exceptions are relatively rare. The Brandon Inn and the Brookfield town hall are a bit out of scale, the former with four stories and the latter with three. There are a few other instances where buildings are notably longer, and this can change the character of the area. The most striking examples are in Brandon, with the commercial row next to the inn, the supermarket, and the long office building for the Ayrshire breeders.

Quality of Architecture

Finally, most of these towns have an unusually high quality of architecture, and this naturally becomes one of the basic elements of environmental quality in the towns. (Note that this is the only one of the major elements of amenity where some subjective judgment is involved.) The architecture prevailing in Vermont in the early nineteenth and mid-nineteenth century—much of which remains today—is more likely to appeal to the average taste than most current new construction. The old structures are mostly in the Georgian, Federal, Greek Revival, Gothic Revival, and Italianate styles (see Appendix A), which tend to appeal to the average person nowadays. During this

Uniform scale of buildings along Main Street, Grafton. Note that buildings all present their gable ends to the street.

The Town House on the hill, Strafford

The Equinox House, Manchester

The Grafton Inn, Grafton

The South Royalton House

period, most building was done by hand, so that each house has its own "personality" and is not a mere assemblage of machine-made parts, as tends to be the case today.

OTHER SIGNIFICANT AMENITIES

No Heavy Traffic

Another major amenity in most of these towns is the lack of heavy traffic passing through. Almost all the smaller towns are fortunate in this respect; the scene is usually quiet and peaceful, with no heavy trucks rolling by. About a dozen of these towns are so remote that relatively little traffic comes through, and ten more have been bypassed.[13] However, several of the larger towns do have heavy traffic, particularly during certain seasons, and have suffered severely. The impact on land use has usually been quite serious, especially in Brandon; yet in some instances, as in Old Bennington and in the central part of Woodstock, much of the older quality has almost miraculously survived.

Limited Commercial Facilities

Many of these towns have limited commercial facilities, usually a "Mom-and-Pop"-type general store, which, of course, means that a lot of residents do their shopping elsewhere. A few actually have no commercial facilities at all, including Old Bennington, Craftsbury Common, and Thetford Hill.[14] The local general store is normally an important element in the local townscape, a natural focal point yet not particularly intrusive (as in Norwich); its architecture usually does not set it sharply apart from the rest of the town. On the other hand, the larger towns naturally have quite a variety of shops, as in Brandon, Chester, Stowe, Woodstock, and Weston. Norwich is different in this respect with relatively few stores but a large number of offices in what were originally houses.

In some instances, the commercial establishments occur predominantly in converted buildings that were previously residences. This is especially obvious in Chester, where a row of such buildings extends along the narrow green at the central point of the town; but it is also quite apparent in East Poultney, Grafton, Stowe, and in most of the office buildings in Norwich.

A related point is equally important. Increased automotive traffic has a lot to do with the principal threats to townscape. The most serious of these is the invasion of the central focal areas by automotive service facilities, which tend to be ugly and messy. (The garages are usually referred to as "heavy commercial" and are always one of the principal problems in protecting residential areas.) In some towns, a commercial garage has appeared right in the center, as in Chelsea and Middletown Springs, and

The grocery and tavern just off the common, East Poultney

Floyd's Store in Randolph Center is in a converted house and (except for the Texaco sign) is unobtrusive.

A cinder block garage facing the common in Middletown Springs

Middletown Springs opposite the garage (see previous photo)

KEVIN EATON

Heavy commercial garage intruding on the view from the North Common in Chelsea

there are several examples along the main street in Brandon; the visual impact is appalling.[15] However, in most towns, auto service facilities are located out of sight from the best part of town, either at the ragged-edge entrance to town or in another village. Such facilities provide necessary services, of course, and have to be located somewhere, but placing them is one of the principal planning problems facing towns in Vermont, as it is all over the country.

Landscaping

Landscaping naturally plays a major role in amenity in these towns, particularly in cases where trees are old and large and where there are deep setbacks. Several of the towns are located amid large trees, and the effect is quite majestic, as in Old Bennington, Dorset, Newfane, Randolph Center, and Thetford Hill. Several towns have deep setbacks along the principal street; clearly defined rows of trees extend for a considerable distance, and the houses are set further back, as in Dorset, Manchester, Randolph Center, and on Park Street in Brandon. Obviously, these streets would look totally different if the trees were not there.

No Incompatible Architecture

Another major element of amenity in most of these towns is the general lack of strikingly incompatible architecture. Most of the towns contain a variety of architectural styles, in the sense in which the term is used by architectural historians, but there is usually a pleasing harmony of scale and texture. In many of the towns, the predominant building type (both residential and institutional) is a white clapboard building with green shutters. This is especially dominant in southern Vermont, as in Manchester, Dorset, and, most strikingly, in Newfane. In most of the towns, some red brick buildings (usually also with green shutters) provide variety, as do the occasional plain white, yellow, or dark red wooden buildings. Sometimes, bright varied colors dominate, particularly in northern Vermont, as in Stowe, Hyde Park, and Montgomery. This may reflect the French Canadian influence. However, the pattern does appear to a limited extent further south, in Chelsea, Chester, Norwich, and South Royalton.

A Sense of Enclosure

In contrast to the towns where the surrounding open areas extend right up to the main street, a larger group of these towns have a central area enclosed by buildings, giving a sense of clearly defined space. This is evident in Chelsea, Manchester, Norwich, Orwell, Weston, and Woodstock. Perhaps the most satisfying sense of enclosure is present in Newfane, where the center consists of a green bisected by the main road; in the middle of the larger (western) half is the fine county courthouse, and also on that side are several other institutional buildings (two inns, a meeting hall, and

Double rows of trees defining the open space along Main Street, Randolph Center

The road up to the Bennington Battle Monument lined by trees, Old Bennington

Newfane has a particularly satisfying sense of enclosure, with the long dimensions of the buildings emphasizing the outer boundary.

The gap at the southeast corner of the park (common) in South Royalton. The rest of the common is tightly enclosed.

Dirt lane along the common in Thetford Hill. The lack of paving emphasizes the rural quality of the town.

TOM HOBAN

a church). The buildings that form the outer boundary of the enclosed space all have their long dimension parallel to that boundary, increasing the sense of enclosure. On the other hand, a gap in the surrounding buildings can look something like a missing tooth. In South Royalton, a gap in enclosure at the southeast corner of the green, along the Central Vermont tracks and adjoining the inn, illustrates the point.

A Lack of Clutter

Most of these towns have so far been spared the urban clutter so common in American cities generally. Major exceptions include the maze of overhead wires and multiple road signs (often with some repeating identical information) that infringe on the best views in several towns. A few towns have been able to put the wires underground in the central areas (as in Woodstock and Manchester), but that is an expensive process. Multiple monuments and monuments carelessly placed (as in Chester) can also give a sense of clutter.

Special Features

As part of the great variety in these towns, a number have striking special features. In several instances, barns are clearly evident right on the main street, as in Chester, Chelsea, Thetford Hill, and Strafford. In some of the more rural towns, some streets are unpaved, as in Thetford Hill, the main street in Brookfield, and Mountain Avenue, the most pleasant street in Woodstock. Brookfield is picturesque primarily because it is located next to a lake, with the well-known floating bridge serving as the only crossing of the lake. In several towns, front porches are quite in evidence, as in Manchester, Grafton, Montgomery, and Peru; and second-floor recessed balconies are frequent in Chester and Grafton.

While spacing between buildings is usually generous enough to preserve the open feeling, single-family-detached housing is by no means the universal rule in good townscape; for example, several attached houses are right on Woodstock Green.

LOCAL ATTITUDES TO TOWNSCAPE

The analysis of the prime elements in Vermont townscape leaves a different question. How do the residents of Vermont towns view their own townscape? In two arbitrarily selected towns,[16] it was possible through interviews to explore how Vermonters looked at their townscape. In testing the assumptions of the study, we can conclude the following.

First, Vermonters tend to treat the town common and the public institutions surrounding the common as the center of town, even if the common and its institutions

The floating bridge, Brookfield

KEVIN EATON

This house with a recessed balcony shows an architectural feature less frequently found outside Vermont.
(For other Vermont architectural specialties, see Appendix A.)

Attached houses along Woodstock Green

are not the focus of social activities. Second, Vermonters identified as important some, but not all, of the amenity characteristics identified above. Most felt that the small scale of the buildings, the open land of the surrounding hills, and the integrity of the town common itself were important amenities. Less agreement existed about uniformity of color of buildings and the necessity of having open space within close proximity to the town's central street.

Third, in some of the towns, increased traffic was viewed as a serious problem. Fourth, town residents appeared to support the notion of town planning aimed at preserving the important attractive features of the town. They supported general beautification efforts and voluntary historic preservation. Most supported height controls for buildings around the town common and controls against further erosion of common space for parking. A majority supported strip zoning controls.

A smaller number of interviews carried out in Stowe revealed some clear-cut indications of prevailing attitudes in one of the major tourist towns. The most striking point, underlined by almost all of the respondents in Stowe, is a sharp distinction between the part of the town regarded by residents primarily as their own—the old downtown area along Main Street—and the part regarded as primarily for tourist use—the Mountain Road toward Mount Mansfield. The obvious corollary is that the local people want to keep their downtown area much as it has been, without major change.

A question on what are the important parts of town also brought consistent answers. Almost all the respondents referred to the ski development on Mount Mansfield (and nearby) as essential to the town's livelihood and as necessary to tourists, but incidentally as useful in various ways for the local people as well. In the downtown area, almost everybody mentioned the library as performing several important civic functions, the post office as a place where people often met, and the white church as playing a substantial symbolic role. (Stowe has no common.) The fact that the high school had been moved way off into the woods was noted several times. The residents strongly stated that they did not want "new style" buildings to replace existing ones along Main Street, and there was considerable discussion about the varied colors of the buildings that are there.

A few respondents stated more explicitly that they were in favor of "historic preservation" without indicating details, and in a couple of instances, residents stated that design control was needed. The lack of a local common was duly noted and deplored, but there was general recognition that it would be difficult to find a place for one in this built-up area. The severe traffic problems on the main street and the Mountain Road were noted by several respondents, and some specifically indicated the need for a bypass to relieve this situation.

Considerable attention was paid in the interviews to the vistas of nearby open space from the downtown area and the importance of protecting them. However, several respondents noted there may be cheaper ways to preserve this than actually buying the land and keeping it in public ownership, either in fee or by the development rights, but they were not able to indicate what these ways would be.

Finally, several respondents took the view that some of the commercial development along the Mountain Road was unattractive compared to the rest of the town. Some noted the recent development of condominiums and especially time-sharing arrangements with the suggestion that their number should be limited.

Notes

1. As indicated above, there are a few exceptions. Three towns are located on a ridgetop (Old Bennington, Craftsbury Common, and Randolph Center) with magnificent views of distant mountain ranges. Five are on a sloping hillside (Danville, Grafton, Middletown Springs, Peacham, and Thetford Hill) but with substantial hills noticeable in the middle distance (except in Danville).

Edmund Bacon has pointed out the importance of the converse situation in the Italian hill towns. The small park at the lower end of the main street in Perugia has a commanding view across the Tiber Valley to Assisi; an opening at the lower end of the main square in Todi provides a vista over the same valley. See E. N. Bacon, *Design of Cities* (1974) at 98.

2. In other instances, substantial hills are in view but only in certain directions, as notably in Norwich and East Poultney (in these cases, to the northeast and southeast only). Similarly, in Brandon, the main range of the Green Mountains lies to the east, with flat land to the west in the Champlain Valley.

3. Moreover, in a few towns, the main street runs off at right angles from the main highway through town, as in Dorset, Plymouth, and Thetford Hill. This has the advantage of keeping through traffic off the local main street. A few towns are obviously located at a crossroads, as in East Poultney and Middletown Springs; in a number of others, as in Grafton, Orwell, and Randolph Center, streets go off in both directions at right angles to the main street, but these are offset, so there is no single crossroads. A few towns are located at a noticeable Y-fork in the road, as in Chester, Norwich, Peru, and Stowe.

4. This is particularly evident in East Poultney and South Woodstock but also occurs in Brookfield, Craftsbury Common, Grafton, Hyde Park, Dorset, Middletown Springs, Newfane, Orwell, Peru, Plymouth, Randolph Center, Strafford, Thetford Hill, and Weston.

5. John W. Reps, *The Making of Urban America* (1965), *passim*.

6. In a good example of secondary focal points, cited by Reps (at 132), the two principal early churches in Woodstock are located at two of the prime sites in town—one at the inner end of Pleasant Street, the main eastern entrance to town, and the other off the western end of the Green.

7. The reverse comment was Gertrude Stein's famous remark about Oakland: "There is no there, there," often quoted with reference to Los Angeles.

8. Sometimes, the focal point can be located more specifically, as, for example, at the Town House (a former church) on the hill at the north end of the green in Strafford.

9. In Hyde Park, the county courthouse is located at a central point, with other facilities right nearby.

10. In Newbury and Weston, the church is near but not right on the common; in East Poultney, one church is within the common.

11. In view of its historical importance, the inn will be regarded as an institutional building rather than a commercial one. In Grafton and Norwich, the inn is at a more central point, and the common is a bit off-center.

12. The minor commercial is often a "Mom-and-Pop"-type general store. This total does not include some previously vacant commercial buildings in Manchester and a funeral parlor in Craftsbury Common. The store in Montgomery is near the common but does not face it.

13. Five of these towns have been bypassed by the interstate—Brookfield, Norwich, Newbury, South Royalton, and Randolph Center. (However, Route 5 continues to take a lot of traffic through Norwich.) Manchester has just been bypassed by the construction of a new limited-access version of Route 7 extending north from Bennington to Route 11 east of Manchester. Four other small towns have been relieved by special local bypasses—Peru, Plymouth, Hyde Park, and Craftsbury Common (bypassed by a road down the valley).

14. An attempt to introduce a small general store in Thetford Hill resulted in considerable community debate. A conditional use permit for this purpose was obtained; but the developer, faced with the prospect of litigation by neighbors, dropped the idea.

15. Occasionally, the reverse situation has prevailed. Two filling stations have closed down on the main street in Woodstock: one has been converted into a rather attractive furniture store and the other, with the addition of a gable roof, into an insurance office.

16. Chelsea, one of the poorer towns, and Dorset, one of the most gentrified.

Chapter 5

Special Problems of the Larger Towns (Is This the Future for Everybody?)

Five of the thirty Vermont towns are notably larger than the rest—Brandon, Chester, Norwich, Stowe, and Woodstock;[1] these have several distinctive characteristics in common that set them apart from the rest.

In part, these distinctive characteristics are merely the natural result of being larger, and they are larger because of some feature in their location that has encouraged growth, be it a site located on some main transportation route or some other special advantage. Analysis of the problems involved in these towns will shed some light on the problems likely to be encountered when and if some of the smaller and more remote towns start to grow on a similar scale.

THE EDGES

Historically, most Vermont towns have had a clearly defined edge beyond which there was nothing but farmland and forest. The existence of such an edge has been one of the prime elements of amenity in such towns. Anyone growing up in town knew that, within a five-minute walk, it was possible to be out in open country. Conversely, for anyone approaching such a town, the first impression is important, as are the continuing impressions on the way in.

In the smaller towns, the situation remains essentially untouched; the town stops sharply at a defined edge in Thetford Hill, Craftsbury Common, Randolph Center, Strafford, and so on. The larger towns (and a few of the smaller) have a different problem. Perhaps the most unattractive feature of recent development in Vermont has been the growth of typical messy commercial strips on the main roads leading out of town, with garages, open car sales lots, motels, filling stations, fast-food joints, and all sorts of dreary buildings making the entrance/exit to the town not a thing of beauty but rather a horror.

Route 4 going east out of Woodstock is a typical example, but plenty of others occur all over the state. The commercial development in Manchester Center is advancing down Route 7A (no longer the main highway) into pristine Manchester village, with the full encouragement of zoning in the latter. A different (and more common) pattern is apparent in Stowe, where Route 100 both north and south of town and Route 108

96

to the north and west are gradually being developed with scattered tourist-oriented commercial establishments of all kinds, but quite different from the concentrated development at the edge of Woodstock.

HEAVY TRAFFIC

The most obvious special characteristic of the larger towns is that all are located on one or more main roads and, therefore, are plagued with heavy traffic, particularly at certain times of the year. In Brandon and Woodstock, the main route goes right through the center of town: Route 4 in Woodstock is the main east/west route across the central part of the state (with an annual average daily traffic of 6,440).[2] Moreover, Route 9 going through Old Bennington (right along the green) has 6,800.[3] Both towns have suffered heavy damage from this kind of traffic.

A different situation exists in two other large towns: a heavily traveled road touches the edge of the central areas and then turns off. Stowe has had the heaviest traffic of all: Route 100 goes right through (with an average daily traffic of 7,150), but the even more traveled Route 108 ("The Mountain Road" to Mount Mansfield and the ski areas, with an average of 7,210) turns off right at the center of town. In Norwich, Route 5 comes close to the center of town and then turns off, passing the main group of community facilities and some of the finer residential areas.[4]

Each of these towns has some special characteristics that contribute to this heavy traffic. Norwich is in part a dormitory town for the faculty of Dartmouth College, located across the river in Hanover, New Hampshire. Both Stowe and Woodstock are among the largest resort towns (and transient tourist centers) in the state, particularly during the fall foliage season and the winter ski season and also to a considerable extent in July and August. Stowe is one of the largest resorts in the state with the massive ski development at Mount Mansfield. Woodstock, where America's ski tows originated, is now a relatively minor ski town, since only one ferocious nearby hill still has a ski tow.

MIXED LAND USE

The most obvious consequence of the heavy traffic in these towns is a striking mixture of commercial and residential land use, quite unlike anything in the smaller towns. Naturally, these towns have a large commercial area at the center, sometimes with attached buildings and considerable scattering of commercial establishments, primarily along the main route of traffic through town. A good deal of blight results.

Brandon provides a striking example of what is likely to happen to land use along heavily traveled main roads in the absence of basic planning plus careful zoning protection. Route 7 (the main north and south highway in the western half of the state) runs right through the middle of Brandon; in this situation, there is naturally a need for some automotive service establishments. The principal business district in Brandon consists of a solid row of commercial buildings, mostly attached and extending north from the Brandon Inn, around the corner and down a small hill, across the brook, and as far as Prospect Street. All this is perfectly normal commercial development for a town the size of Brandon, and raises no serious planning questions.

The problems occur on the remaining Route 7 frontage from Prospect Street to the northern edge of the settled area, a distance of about half a mile. Along this stretch, the east frontage consists first of a group of some half-dozen fine houses, with a smaller number on the west side, followed on the east side by three filling stations, with a supermarket, a church, a small park, and some houses on the west side. Continuing north, there is about a quarter-mile of good houses on both sides, ending up at the north end of the settled area with a filling station and a garage on the west side. This garage and all these filling stations (except the one last mentioned)[5] were in place before zoning. The first group of houses is zoned Neighborhood Residential, but the local policy is to permit commercial development along the Route 7 frontage in the upper part of Brandon, presumably because of the heavy traffic passing by; the upper Route 7 frontage is zoned to permit this as of right.

If enough demand existed in Brandon for automotive services (and/or other commercial services) to fill up this entire area with that kind of development, Brandon would then have a strip commercial area extending for about a mile north and south along its main street. This might not be very handsome, but apart from that, it would not do much harm. In fact, the market has taken up and put to commercial use only about one-quarter of this frontage on both sides. The result is that a substantial number of people are living on this frontage, some in fine houses, with filling stations interspersed between the houses. Not many people really want to have a filling station or garage next to their house; and no one will argue that this is the way to enhance good Vermont townscape. However, these establishments are not open in the evenings, and the friction inevitable in a mixed-land-use situation like this has apparently been reduced by the self-policing that is possible in small towns. In addition, expansion by an addition on a commercial lot (already including a filling station and various service establishments) has been permitted by a side yard variance, within a few feet of one of the houses.

The story of Brandon is not unusual, but it has left quite a lot of people living in fine houses uncomfortably situated next to filling stations and garages. It is because of sheer good luck, more than municipal foresight, that the same thing did not happen before zoning on Woodstock Green or in many other places in Vermont towns.

Woodstock does have somewhat similar problems, however, for the same reasons. The finest parts of town have somehow survived with few physical changes, although

Commercial alternating with residential along Main Street, Brandon

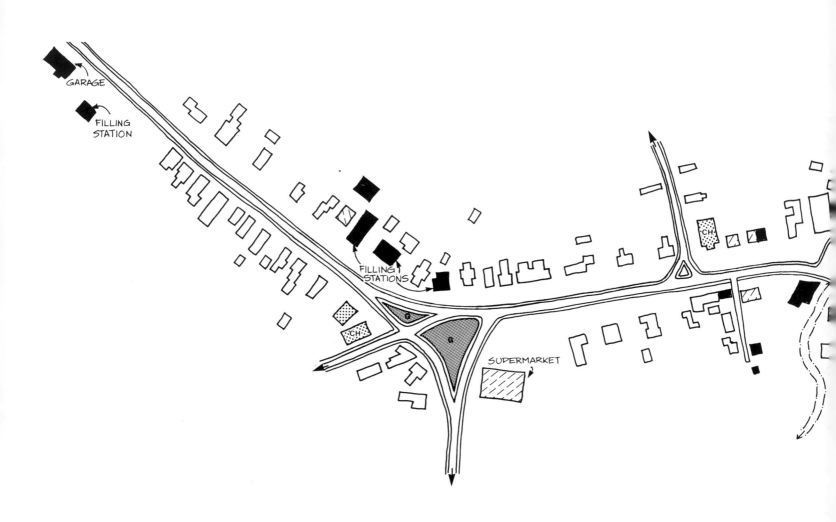

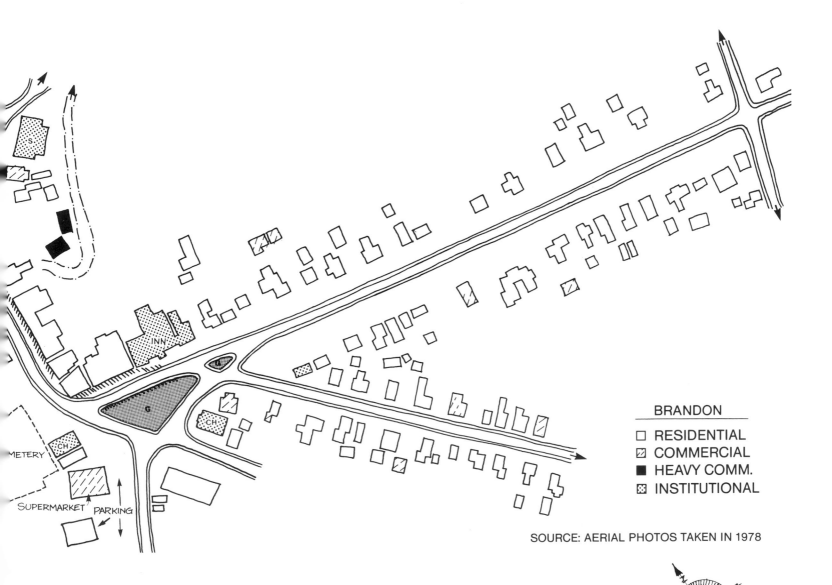

BRANDON

☐ RESIDENTIAL
▨ COMMERCIAL
■ HEAVY COMM.
▩ INSTITUTIONAL

SOURCE: AERIAL PHOTOS TAKEN IN 1978

the Route 4 frontage now naturally has some problems as a residential area. The "downstreet" area is a solidly developed center around the square, gradually extending east along Central Street (Route 4). At Lincoln Street, this development stops abruptly and for the next few hundred feet, a solid residential area has survived intact, followed by a lesser scatteration of mostly commercial establishments within the area originally (pre-1930) dominated by the old Woodstock railway station.[6] Beyond the edge of town, Route 4 east includes an even messier commercial strip.

In Stowe and Chester, the pattern is quite different: residential buildings that originally dominated the main street have mostly been converted to commercial use or occasionally replaced by a new commercial building. As a result, the main street now contains a mixture of residential, commercial, and community facilities scattered along the frontage, with no real focal point. In Norwich, the main community facilities remain concentrated along the green near the right-angle bend in Route 5; the main street nearby is dominated by office buildings (formerly houses) plus some retail establishments and the Norwich Inn. Peripheral development continues from Route 5 north along the River Road.

The impact of these changes, deriving primarily from the heavy through traffic, varies among the different towns. The resulting problems are particularly evident in Brandon (which provides a classic example of what American urban planning tries most to avoid—heavy commercial alternating with fine residences). The east end of Woodstock is not much better, but Woodstock has been singularly fortunate in the preservation of the high quality of both residences and community facilities along the Green.[7] In Stowe and Chester, the result has been a destruction of most of the sense of a focal point.

OTHER RESIDENTIAL STREETS

Since these five towns are larger, they have more complex street patterns, unlike the usual single street where open land remains right behind the buildings on both sides. Separate residential neighborhoods are usually located on other streets, parallel or intersecting.

In some of these larger towns, the other streets away from the main road include some of the most attractive development, just because they are farther away from the traffic. The situation is clearest in Woodstock and Brandon, where the main traffic route goes right through the center of town. In Woodstock, in sharp contrast to the heavy traffic on Route 4, other streets are relatively unaffected: River Street and Mountain Avenue across the river retain high residential quality with relatively little traffic; Elm Street going north, which carries medium traffic, is even better. Again, Park Street in Brandon, running south from the inn, is one of the most beautiful streets in the state and relatively untouched by the traffic on Route 7.[8] Since the heaviest traffic around Norwich is carried either on the interstate or on Route 5 into town, the main street running north from Route 5 carries relatively little traffic (it does not go anywhere) and retains high quality.

The question naturally arises whether, in view of the strong pressures for decentralization, it might be desirable to encourage some more concentrated commercial development, i.e., a medium-size shopping center, at some location outside some of the larger towns. In a small town, there is no problem; the single store (if there is one) takes care of daily needs, and people do a lot of their shopping elsewhere. In the larger towns, this problem is a serious one and keeps coming up repeatedly. In Woodstock, attempts have been made to develop a rival commercial center both in West Woodstock and at the eastern end of Woodstock village. The potential for running a traditional downtown by encouraging a new outer shopping center, presumably because the latter is a "good ratable," is one of the most familiar stories in present-day America. If, however, a situation arises where a new outer commercial facility is appropriate, it is, of course, important that the site be selected carefully and preferably in advance.

WHERE DO THE LESS ATTRACTIVE USES GO?

A number of land uses do not (or may not) fit into traditional Vermont townscape but, nonetheless, are needed somewhere in all but the smallest towns. These include automotive services, motels, some retail commercial, and some forms of inexpensive housing. Having these in a convenient location is especially important for less mobile residents and the less wealthy generally; this is an important consideration in local planning. If these uses are to be excluded from a historic district at the center, and preferably also from a conspicuous location at the main entrance, where are they to go?

The question cannot be answered in detail for these thirty towns, yet the general guiding principle is clear enough. Such uses should be in some convenient location that is not right in the midst of the traditional townscape, and preferably not visible from any residential areas. Where that is can be determined only by detailed planning for each town.

Automotive Services

Garages, filling stations, and auto sales lots are almost inherently obtrusive, and so these are the most important uses to keep out of good townscape. The same is true of other "heavy commercial" uses, such as building material yards. The danger is all too clearly illustrated by the garages located right at the main corner in Chelsea and Middletown Springs; the scattering of such uses along the main streets of Brandon and

Federally subsidized housing for the elderly on Pleasant Street, Woodstock

Chester indicates the extent of the problem on main highways in the larger towns. It is a major planning problem in Vermont and elsewhere to find a location for them that is convenient but unobtrusive. A particularly difficult problem arises in connection with downtown parking areas, which may have a similar impact, yet by definition have to be next to (or near) downtown.

Retail Commercial

All but four of the thirty towns have some retail commercial facilities, usually located right near the center and usually unobtrusive, often in formerly residential buildings or other buildings that look that way. Nothing contained herein would suggest that this is undesirable; the pattern is familiar and long established. However, at least in the larger towns, having some duplicating facilities has the advantage (especially for low-income residents) of competitive pricing. These would presumably be in modern commercial buildings that need to go somewhere, but not necessarily in the traditional townscape.

Inexpensive Housing

The situation is both different and more important with respect to low-cost and moderate-cost housing. In a time of surging housing prices, almost every town has a shortage of such inexpensive housing; such housing is acutely needed if many Vermonters are to have the precious opportunity of staying in their hometown.

Vermont is one of the few states where statute law points strongly in this direction. The Planning Act requires that mobile homes be treated like other forms of housing.[9] If a town violates this provision—or violates a more general statutory exhortation to plan for all types of housing[10]—any persons aggrieved may call on the attorney general to represent them in challenging this.[11] Under another law, mobile home parks are encouraged,[12] but are to locate in an area screened by woods from other development, i.e., not in the central part of town.

Moreover, while mobile homes now provide new and inexpensive housing, other opportunities do exist. In many towns, there is no legal reason why large older houses cannot be subdivided into small apartments anywhere in town, including the best townscape.[13] This is already happening in some towns. There is, of course, no reason why relatively inexpensive new housing need be ugly. For example, some public housing projects have fitted easily into traditional New England towns; some even consist of freestanding white clapboard buildings.

What little experience is immediately available suggests that the problem may not be insoluble, at least for the larger towns, where it is most important. In Woodstock, a fine brick house on Pleasant Street within (but near the edge of) the area of the best townscape has recently been converted to a federally subsidized low-rent apartment building for the elderly, with widespread public support; an addition at the rear (not readily visible from the street) was subsequently added. Many people in town are quite proud of this; most strangers don't know it's there. Further east on the same street, there is a half-mile of frontage (a quarter-mile on each side) largely developed with miscellaneous commercial establishments (for example, an office to place orders for Sears Roebuck), many of them in converted residences.

Proceeding further east (and around the corner) to the edge of town, there is an unhandsome commercial strip along Route 4 east; a substantial and rather attractive small shopping center ("Woodstock East") is located off the road uphill; and a much larger commercial-industrial area is below and along the river. Neither is really visible from the road. Plenty of commercial land is available without intruding on the traditional townscape.

Underlying the entire problem, of course, is the need for careful long-range planning in all of the towns. At the least, all should have an adopted comprehensive town plan, preferably followed with zoning controls and historic districts.

Notes

1. The township population figures are as follows: Brandon, 4,194; Woodstock, 3,124; Stowe, 2,991; Chester, 2,791; and Norwich, 2,398. Only two involve separately organized villages: Woodstock village has a population of 1,178 and Stowe village has 531.

2. In a more recent traffic study made during foliage season in the fall of 1984, the traffic on Route 4 in Woodstock was the highest in the entire state, with an average daily figure (for all of October) of 11,113. See *Rutland Herald*, December 5, 1984, p. 7. The figure for July 1985 was about 11,800.

3. Chester has examples of both patterns: Route 11 goes right through but with far less traffic (3,020), and Route 103 (another main route across the state but on a diagonal) touches the east end of town and then turns north up through Chester Depot (with 3,160).

4. Norwich has been bypassed by Interstate 91, but the traffic on Route 5 remains quite heavy.

5. In the case of this filling station, Brandon attempted to resist commercial development on Route 7 without success, because of the perceived likelihood of traffic problems. A permit was sought for the filling station in 1975, but was denied; the developers successfully challenged denial of the permit on the ground that the Brandon authorities had not provided the required period for notice of hearing under the Vermont statutes. Because the denial of a permit was held invalid, Brandon was without zoning protection for a while; before an interim zoning ordinance was passed, the filling station developers managed to build enough so that they had vested rights.

6. This area cannot be said to have gone way downhill; it was never uphill. Because of the location of the railroad station (and yards), it has always been heavy commercial in character and, in fact, partly industrial.

7. The village was not zoned until about 1970, and for many years (after the old Methodist church was torn down), a vacant lot remained right on the Green, as if to invite a filling station to move in. For-

tunately, the hole (and another one across the street) were finally filled, one by moving a house from elsewhere and the other by new construction.

8. There is a striking story involving Park Street. A wealthy woman from the West bought a large part of this whole area, leased out the houses to tenants strictly of her own choice, and then in her will left each house to the resident tenant.

9. 24 Vt. Stats. Ann., Ch. 117, Sec. 4406(4)(A).

10. *Id*. at Sec. 4406(4)(b) and Sec. 4383(C).

11. *Id*. at Sec. 4445(a).

12. 10 Vt. Stats. Ann., Ch. 153, Sec. 6201 *et seq*.

13. Strong market pressures encourage owners to make such apartments more expensive.

Chapter 6

How to Protect and Enhance Townscape— Legal Considerations

In most of the thirty Vermont towns, a silent compact among the residents spans two centuries of shared experience that acts to preserve and protect the fragile townscape resource. Nevertheless, this compact can break down in the face of threats characteristic to most towns in Vermont. The threats to townscape can be summarized as follows.

THREATS TO TOWNSCAPE

Unchecked Population Growth

Population growth (the "baby boom") and increases in income and leisure time, together with the availability of fast and easy transportation via Interstates 89 and 91, are inevitably leading to increased traffic and so to congestion in Vermont towns—and also to various kinds of new development that take up what was previously open space and which may or may not fit in with the traditional townscape. New off-street parking facilities, often without landscaping, and automobile servicing areas pose a particularly serious problem, but conventional buildings such as post offices may also detract from the traditional image.

Strip Development

The development of ribbon commercial strips on the approaches to historic towns is perhaps the worst blot on traditional Vermont townscape. Moreover, pressures toward decentralization of both commercial and community facilities, to get better space and more parking, are tending to tear apart the fabric of the historic downtowns.

Highway Design

Highway "improvements" and, particularly, the failure to build traffic bypasses around historic towns can deal devastating blows to traditional townscape. To date, the planning process in the State Transportation Department has not usually emphasized scenic townscape.

Reforestation

The ecology of Vermont tends toward reforestation with the consequent loss of open hillsides and of scenic vistas generally.

Lack of Low-income Housing and Gentrification

In towns where gentrification is proceeding apace, housing is becoming increasingly unavailable to the local population and their children. Some may be forced out, with considerable loss to the opportunities for democratic living; there are also various implications for townscape with the spread of modular and mobile homes. Moreover, as tourism increases, the traditional downtowns in the most popular towns are increasingly given over to expensive boutiques and gift shops, which sell nothing of any use to the resident population. The result is an inherently unstable pattern of retailing, leading to constant turnover (and new signs) and tending to drive out long-established local services.

PROTECTION AND ENHANCEMENT

Assuming that the appearance of our physical environment is one of our most precious assets, what is to be done? In some instances, action is needed to prevent the destruction of present values; yet no drastic changes in the existing townscape are needed or appropriate. However, in many instances, various minor problems have arisen in the towns discussed herein, and perhaps more so in other towns that are generally similar, as pleasant features have been lost (trees dying off) or minor obtrusive elements have come in; therefore, real opportunities exist to enhance as well as to protect what is already first-rate.

Enhancement of the towns in these cases is often as simple as replacing trees, repairing benches and walkways, and removing sign clutter. In other instances, protection and enhancement of Vermont townscape is likely to involve at least some legal measures, and so the probable legal problems need to be considered.

The Legal Basis of Protection

The legal basis for protecting historic townscape has been established in American law for decades. In fact, even back in the early 1940s, this notion was tested in the most critical type of case; regulation of private property rights evoked enthusiastic judicial acceptance. In the first cases from New Orleans, the courts quite consciously adopted the broader of two possible interpretations of an ambiguous enabling provision in the Louisiana state constitution, so as to subject to the aesthetic restrictions not merely selected landmark buildings but the entire Vieux Carre.[1]

The courts have long been concerned with the tricky problems involved in aesthetic regulation generally, and have gradually worked out a rather sensible rationale in dealing with them. Back at the turn of the century, aesthetic regulations were considered invalid; that is to say, such matters were regarded as none of the government's business.[2] However, as usual, when established legal doctrine comes into conflict with a strongly felt need, the latter prevailed; the towns kept on passing such regulations and the courts soon adopted the doctrine that aesthetic considerations could provide one valid basis for police power regulations so long as some more conventional considerations (involving health or safety) were also present.

Once this "big brother" theory was adopted, legal fiction flowered vigorously, and it was soon discovered that sign restrictions were really concerned with health and safety factors; after all, a billboard might blow over and hit somebody, or criminals might find safety behind the friendly shelter of a billboard.[3] Ever since the 1930s, the courts have been moving steadily toward a broader and more realistic acceptance of aesthetic restrictions. A variety of intermediate rationales have been developed for this purpose, including an economics-plus-aesthetics one (actually, a variant of the "big brother" theory). Under this theory, a fine townscape (or landscape) will appeal to tourists and so is an important part of the economic base of an area.

However, the courts have usually and quite reasonably stopped just short of full acceptance of aesthetics, for an obvious and quite valid reason: in many instances, aesthetic judgments involve matters where there can be reasonable differences in opinion, so that the power to regulate in such situations would involve arbitrary use of discretion. At the present time, the courts can usually be counted on to uphold aesthetic regulations in two situations:

1. If the activity restricted (e.g., a junkyard) is clearly regarded as obnoxious and ugly by a broad segment of the population, particularly in contrast to an attractive background. When such a situation is clearly presented, the courts feel no need to worry their heads about how to deal with the marginal cases where differences of opinion can reasonably arise.[4]
2. In cases involving required conformity to a prevailing and distinctive architectural style, for in this situation, the guidelines for determining conformity (based on the characteristics of the style) are clear enough to provide policy guidance for those administering it.

A fairly specific definition of the important elements of Vermont townscape is thus important not only as a matter of substance, so that we may know what needs to be done, but also for legal reasons, so that what we decide to do is likely to be upheld. In recent years, when the courts are required to pass on land use regulations, they have

110

been looking rather carefully into what is really involved; in this mood, they are not likely to look kindly on vaguely phrased regulations.[5]

Aesthetic regulation should provide clearly understandable standards; this fits into a broader general trend in the law. Since the courts are now seriously concerned with inquiring as to what is really going on, they are more likely to insist on some fairly definite standards, rather than approving a situation where an agency is told to go and solve the problem on its own by doing the right thing, making good use of its discretion. In other words, we should anticipate a revival of the legal doctrine against delegation of legislative power, with no adequate standards and guidelines for the administrators. As anyone who follows the advance sheets knows, we are now seeing exactly that, a revival of the delegation-of-power doctrine.

APPROACHES TO PROTECTING TOWNSCAPE

Speaking generally, under the American legal system, there are five kinds of action that are available to protect endangered values.

First, basic land use planning to guide the processes of change toward a more desirable (yet realistic) future pattern of agricultural, forest, residential, commercial, and industrial land use, and to provide the necessary public infrastructure at the appropriate time. To be effective, this will require decisions on both what types of use will be appropriate in what kinds of places and just where in town each type of use should go. To take the obvious example, if a town is to cope with threats to its townscape, basic (and difficult) decisions must be made on where to put needed land uses that tend to harm townscape—the necessary parking facilities and the less attractive "heavy commercial" developments (automotive services, building material yards, and the like). The basic planning principle should be to find a place for these somewhere but out of sight, away from prime townscape.

The Vermont planning enabling act[6] is one of the best in the country, and it explicitly provides for such planning as the proper basis on which other legal devices may be developed.

Second, acquisition of land in fee, by either eminent domain or voluntary purchase (or donation), and keeping it in public ownership. Purchase, of course, requires payment of the "fair market value" of the land, and from then on, the public has the responsibility for maintenance. As a modern variant of this, the land so acquired may be resold (perhaps at a loss, as often happens in urban renewal) subject to restrictions (by covenant or otherwise) that will protect the values involved. In traditional terms, any such use of eminent domain must satisfy the constitutional requirement of a "public use." If public funds are used in a voluntary purchase, this can be challenged in a taxpayer's action, and this must satisfy the test of a "public purpose," which has a quite different content.[7]

Third, to restrict the use of land and buildings thereon by regulations adopted under the police power—that is, to leave the land in private ownership but take away some of the development rights without compensation. The familiar example of this is zoning, but other freestanding police-power ordinances are also fairly common, and historic district and landmark designation[8] ordinances have been spreading rapidly. The standard legal justification, stated rather abstractly, is that such regulations must promote public health, safety, morals, and general welfare. Modern land use law consists of translating this abstract principle into more specific rules of law, which can be used to decide concrete cases.

Fourth, the two remedies discussed immediately above are potentially rather drastic and involve real disadvantages; so in recent years a lot of thought has been given to developing various types of intermediate solutions, essentially combining police-power regulations with some form of partial compensation. This could be done in numerous ways. For present purposes, the most promising is simply to divide up the various rights in the well-known "bundle," as between public and private ownership. Fortunately, Vermont has a statute dealing directly with this, authorizing action along these lines at either the state or municipal level and setting forth in some detail the various arrangements by which this can be carried out.[9] Moreover, in many instances, much can be accomplished by persuasion. In fact, in some instances, this is more effective than any of the legal tools.

Fifth, to some extent, what is important in protecting townscape scenery will involve public investment, and this is even more true for its enhancement. For this purpose, the appropriate vehicle is a capital budget spelling out a program for such investment, or whatever takes its place in the smaller Vermont towns.

Not much work has been done on the criteria for choosing between the types of legal tools in the various kinds of situations.[10] The first two types are the ones most commonly used, and these involve both advantages and disadvantages. Normally, the safest way to lock up a precious resource is to put it in public ownership and leave it there. On the other hand, this obviously costs money and also involves public responsibility for continuing maintenance. Moreover, there is always resistance in Vermont to increasing public ownership. Fortunately, for present purposes, this is usually not necessary; in many instances, simple persuasion with perhaps some limited use of legal tools will accomplish what is necessary.

Police-power regulations are, of course, the most commonly used legal tool to implement American planning decisions, primarily (but by no means entirely) through zoning; such a remedy is appropriate in many instances. However, some of the tools needed to preserve scenery involve severe restrictions on land and may come afoul of the general "nationwide rule"—that police-power regulations must leave a property owner with *some* potential use and income from his land (*not* with the most profitable ["highest and best"] use). There are, therefore, definite limits to the extent to which scenery preservation can be accomplished in this way. The use of rights less than fee is thus particularly appropriate in scenic preservation and the enhancement of scenery.

Notes

1. *New Orleans* v. *Pergament*, 198 La. 852, 5 So. 2d 129 (1941).
2. See, for example, *Curran Bill Posting and Distribution Co.* v. *Denver*, 47 Colo. 221, 107 P. 261 (1910).
3. See, particularly, *Thomas Cusack Co.* v. *City of Chicago*, 242 U.S. 526 (1917).
4. That is, courts can at least approve regulation of the lowest common denominator—whatever is widely regarded as aesthetically offensive. See *United Advertising Corp.* v. *Metuchen*, 42 N.J. 1, 198 A.2d 447 (1964).

Professor John Costonis has suggested a wholly different legal basis for legitimate historic preservation regulations in a most stimulating recent article. See Costonis, *Law and Aesthetics: A Critique and a Reformulation of the Dilemmas*, 80 Michigan Law Review 355 (1982). Under this approach, the real function of such restrictions is to protect artifacts that have a rich symbolic significance to many people, in effect as a way of averting cultural disintegration.

5. See *South of Second Associates* v. *Georgetown*, 196 Colo. 89, 580 P.2d 807 (1978); *Morristown Road Associates* v. *Bernardsville*, 163 N.J. Super. 58, 394 A.2d 157 (L. Div. 1978); *A-S-P Associates* v. *City of Raleigh*, 298 N.C. 207, 258 S.E.2d 444 (1979); *Santa Fe* v. *Gamble-Skogmo*, 73 N.M. 410, 389 P.2d 13 (1964); *Cf. Maher* v. *New Orleans*, 516 F.2d 1051 (5th Cir. 1975), *cert. denied*, 426 U.S. 905 (1976).
6. 24 Vt. Stats. Ann., Ch. 117, Sec. 4301 *et seq.*
7. Strictly speaking, the public purpose doctrine has evolved in taxpayers' suits as a means to test the validity of public expenditures at the state and local level, and reached its culmination in *Jones* v. *Portland*, 245 U.S. 217 (1917) and *Green* v. *Frazier*, 253 U.S. 233 (1920), although the requirement there, of a showing of special local conditions, was apparently removed by the per curiam affirmance in *Standard Oil Co.* v. *Lincoln*, 275 U.S. 504 (1927). The public use doctrine, as a limitation on the use of eminent domain, has gone through a long and complex evaluation, involving quite different content— from the restrictive nineteenth-century version (use by a public agency or by most of the public) through a great broadening in the Western irrigation cases, and more of the same in a wide variety of cases on public housing and urban renewal, to a practical withdrawal of judicial review in *Berman* v. *Parker*, 348 U.S. 26 (1954) and succeeding decisions. Unfortunately, the courts have often confused the issue by carelessly using the two phrases interchangeably, as most recently in *Hawaii Housing Authority* v. *Midkiff*, 463 U.S. 1323 (1983).
8. Landmark designation was first authorized in Vermont by Laws 1986, Ch. 243.
9. 10 Vt. Stats. Ann., Sec. 6303 *et seq.*
10. For a first try at this, see Bennington County Regional Planning Commission, *The Vermont River: Heritage and Promise* (1975), ch. 5.

Chapter 7

"Design Control" Ordinances in Vermont

The early authority for historic district ordinances (not including landmark designation) was found in Chapter 117 of the Vermont Planning and Development Act passed in the 1960s. The text of this section reads as follows:

> (6) Design control districts. Zoning regulations may contain provisions for the establishment of design control districts. Prior to the establishment of such a district, the planning commission shall prepare a report describing the particular planning and design problems of the proposed district and setting forth a design plan for the areas which shall include recommended planning and design criteria to guide future development. The planning commission shall hold a public hearing, after public notice, on such report. After such hearing, the planning commission may recommend to the legislative body such design control district. A design control district can be created for any area containing structures of historical, architectural or cultural merit, and other areas in which there is a concentration of community interest and participation such as a central business district, civic center or a similar grouping or focus of activities. Within such a designated design control district no structure may be erected, reconstructed, substantially altered, restored, moved, demolished or changed in use or type of occupancy without approval of the plans therefor by the planning commission. A design review board may be appointed by the legislative body of the municipality to advise the planning commission, which board shall have such term of office, and such procedural rules, as the legislative body determines.[1]

This provision represents a fairly early recognition of the importance of preserving historic values in architecture—the historic preservation movement came into prominence in the 1970s—and has served to make possible some action in Vermont along these lines. However, this language was added to the act fairly late in the course of its drafting, and so was not thoroughly discussed. The title "Design Control" was almost ideally chosen to dissuade Vermonters from having anything to do with it. Moreover, extensive recent experience with historic preservation legislation nationally has brought major improvements.

THE ORDINANCES

Eleven towns in Vermont have design control ordinances. Naturally, some of these towns are among those covered in the main survey (Old Bennington, Guildhall, Manchester, and Woodstock); others were omitted because they are larger cities with quite

114

different problems (Burlington, Winooski, St. Johnsbury, and Montpelier) or for other reasons (Calais, Greensboro, and Wilmington).

Report and Plan

The statute wisely requires a preliminary report plus a special design plan as a basis for action, within the overall context of a plan as the basis for zoning. Not all the existing reports or plans are readily available, nor are they always used for the guidance they could provide. However, some of the ordinances do mention the existence of a plan as the basis for the ordinance (as, for example, in St. Johnsbury). In some instances, the report and/or plan have contained valuable material. For example, the report for Manchester contains an interesting description of the evolution of a Vermont village into an early nineteenth-century summer resort, with the suggestion that the existing architecture in Manchester provides a full record of that transition (and noting that the older estates have been shifting to institutional use). The report for Guildhall suggests that the present town provides a good example of rural prosperity in early nineteenth-century Vermont, with a strong emphasis on Greek Revival buildings. The overall plan for Guildhall (recently readopted) is meticulous and impressive and leads up to the design control provisions. The design plan for Woodstock is unique in spelling out detailed architectural and site planning characteristics varying between different parts of town; for example, High Street is very different from the Green.

Locations

A few of the ordinances contain specific references indicating precisely where they apply. The Burlington ordinance states that it applies in four different types of locations: the "waterfront core," the "regional core," the "inner city," and historic buildings. Moreover, this ordinance sets forth specific policies to be applied in the first and last of these four; the text provides no further mention of the other two. On the waterfront core, those administering the ordinance are instructed to encourage (but not to require) provision for pedestrian access along the lake and also (so far as possible) to encourage additional plazas and greenery in that area—and to pay special attention to the magnificent views across the lake toward the Adirondacks, on behalf of both developments in the waterfront core and those in buildings on higher ground behind. For this purpose, one-story and two-story buildings "are to be desired" along the lake shore, with greater height on the escarpment above. The location of the historic buildings district is spelled out in detail in the text, which contains general criteria of the same sort discussed in relation to other towns below.

The Manchester ordinance states that it applies to all land within the village and contains a special provision (and different arrangements) to deal with the recent rehabilitation of a large, old hotel in the center of the village, the Equinox House. The ordinance in St. Johnsbury states that it is to apply along the main street in the upper level of town, which is the historic area.

Purpose

The values to be protected are explicitly stated first of all in the statute—that the concern should be with areas and structures of "historic, architectural, and cultural merit" together with areas with a concentration of community interest and participation, such as the central business district, civic centers, and with various other groupings of activities. Some of the ordinances (as in Burlington) have simply copied this statutory language into the ordinance. A few others have mentioned other values as well, as with the reference to natural resources in Winooski and the reference to providing pleasure and adding to both the economic base and the tax base in Wilmington.

Criteria

The heart of any historic district ordinance lies in the criteria for evaluating proposed new construction and alterations, and in this respect, the ordinances fall into two quite different groups. A large group of them contain only broad general references (variously expressed) to "compatibility" or "harmony" with the existing pattern; a few ordinances have described the elements of compatibility in considerable detail, generally along the lines of earlier provisions from Savannah, Georgia and Tucson, Arizona.

Among the ordinances with general language, Burlington refers to compatibility of design, texture, and materials. Burlington also contains a reference to preventing the removal or disruption of the city's historic heritage generally. References in Old Bennington and Manchester spell it out a bit more, in terms of appropriateness to the pattern of a New England village and with specific references to exterior appearance and to bulk. Several ordinances use the phrase "harmony" instead of "compatibility." For example, in Montpelier, the ordinance refers to harmony of exterior design with neighboring buildings and then refers to compatibility of exterior materials and landscaping, and then again to preventing incompatible designs, buildings, color, and exterior materials.

Three ordinances drafted for Northeast Kingdom towns refer to harmony of exterior design and to compatibility of exterior materials, landscaping, and exterior color schemes; two also include the Montpelier language about preventing incompatibility. The guiding principle in drafting these provisions seems to be that, if a phrase is vague, it will take on additional meaning by being repeated several times.

The problem in all these ordinances is, of course, how administrators are to define and interpret "compatibility" and "harmony." These ordinances present real problems in terms of the possibility of administration based merely on whim.

116

In sharp contrast, four of the ordinances do provide more specific standards, which give a lot more guidance to those administering them. The Winooski ordinance suggests a comparison of a proposed building or change therein with other neighboring buildings with respect to the scale of buildings and particularly their height, the amount of setback, and several of the standard items often seen in these more specific ordinances: the relation between the height and the width of the facade, the rhythm of solids and voids (doors and windows), the pattern of the height and width of windows, the shape of the roof, the amount of open space and planting around, together with a more general reference to compatibility of materials, texture, and color. The provisions in the Guildhall report are quite similar but add a specific on height (within 15 percent of the average nearby) and consideration of the prevailing spacing between buildings and similarity of materials.

Two other ordinances in Woodstock and Wilmington have more specific provisions, which are set forth below. The Woodstock criteria read as follows:

a. HEIGHT. The height of buildings or alterations shall be considered in relation to the average height of existing adjacent buildings, and the building being constructed or altered.

b. SETBACK. The front, side and rear setbacks shall be considered in relation to the prevailing setback existing in the immediate area.

c. PROPORTION. (1) The relationship between the width and height of the front elevations of adjacent buildings shall be considered in the construction or alteration of a building; (2) The relationship of width to height of windows and doors of adjacent buildings shall be considered in the construction or alteration of a building.

d. PATTERN. (1) Alternating solids and openings (wall to windows and doors) in the front facade of a building create a rhythm observable to viewers. This pattern of solids and openings in the front facade shall be considered in the construction or alteration of a building; (2) Variation of spacing between the buildings in the immediate area shall be considered in the construction or alteration of a building.

e. MATERIALS. The similarity or compatibility of existing materials on the exterior walls or roofs of buildings in the immediate area shall be considered in the construction or alteration of a building. A building or alteration shall be considered to be compatible if the building materials used possess a kind or type which are appropriate in the context of other buildings in the immediate area.

f. ARCHITECTURAL FEATURES. Architectural features, including but not limited to, cornices, windows, shutters, fanlights, entablature, prevailing in the immediate area, shall be considered in the construction or alteration of a building. It is not intended that the details of old buildings be duplicated precisely, but they should be regarded as suggestive of the extent, nature and scale of details that would be appropriate on new buildings or alterations.

g. CONTINUITY. Physical elements such as fences, evergreen masses, or building facades may combine to form lines of continuity along a street. These elements shall be considered in the construction or alteration of a building.

h. DIRECTION OF FRONT FACADE. Structural shape, placement of openings and architectural features give a predominantly vertical, horizontal or angular character to the building's front facade and shall be considered in the construction or alteration of a building.

i. ROOF SHAPE. The similarity or compatibility of roof shapes in the immediate area shall be considered in the construction or alteration of a building.[2]

The elaborate provisions in Wilmington are as follows:

1. SITE CRITERIA
   a. SPATIAL RELATIONSHIPS

   (i) *Front Setback.* Building setbacks from the street should be consistent with setback distances of adjacent buildings.
   (ii) *Side Setbacks.* Side setbacks from adjacent buildings should recognize and complement the rhythm of spacing between existing buildings.
   (iii) *Alignment of Building.* Alignment of directionality of the major axis of a building should be related to the prevailing orientation of adjacent buildings.
   (iv) *Site Organization.* The organization of buildings, drives, parking areas, walks, service areas and other site components should have a functional, safe, and harmonious interrelationship, and be compatible with existing site features and adjacent buildings.

   b. VISUAL APPEARANCE

   (i) *Preservation of Existing Features.* Important site features such as stone walls, street trees, shrubs and other features of the townscape should be preserved.
   (ii) *Site Structures.* New site structures should be of appropriate materials and scale, and be appropriately located in relationship with the site and streetscape.
   (iii) *Planting.* Use of plant materials should be encouraged to provide an overall setting within the streetscape. Plant species should not be highly ornamental and planting composition should be complementary to the scale and style of the building.
   (iv) *Screening.* Storage areas, service areas, trash receptacles, parking areas and similar accessory structures and uses should be screened from street views and adjoining properties.
   (v) *Paving Materials.* Choice of paving materials should consider the need to delineate pedestrian and vehicular areas while maintaining consistency throughout the district.
   (vi) *Continuity.* Physical elements such as building facades, fences, walls and plantings should relate from one site to another to provide overall visual continuity along the street.

2. BUILDING CRITERIA
   a. FORM RELATIONSHIPS

   (i) *Style*. New construction or renovations should be of similar architectural style with that of existing or adjacent properties. For those areas where design compatibility does not exist, it is the intent of the Design Control District to promote architecture of a traditional New England character.

   (ii) *Proportion*. The ratio of height to width of the front elevations of new buildings and additions should be related to existing or adjacent properties.

   (iii) *Roof Type and Pitch*. Similarity in roof style, pitch, and materials should be considered in the planning and design of new buildings. New roof materials on additions should match existing roof materials.

   b. VISUAL APPEARANCE

   (i) *Materials, Texture and Color*. Materials for new construction should be similar to the types and textures of materials used within the District. Renovations, restorations and maintenance work should make every effort to match existing materials and textures. Similarity of color, materials and texture within the District or of the existing structures should be considered in the planning and design of new buildings or renovations. The range of colors should fall within the range established by the Design Review Committee.

   (ii) *Architectural Details*. For new construction, architectural details characteristic of the particular architectural style proposed should be incorporated into the design. It is the intent of these to promote architecture of a traditional New England character in areas where design compatibility does not exist. Renovations should retain existing architectural details. Details should be consistent with the period and style of the architecture involved and should harmoniously relate to adjacent buildings.

   (iii) *Solid to Void Proportions*. The proportion of solids to voids (doors to windows) in the facade of a building establishes a rhythm which is perceived by a person viewing the building. The rhythm of solids to voids should be considered in the design and planning of a building or renovation.

   (iv) *Window and Door Proportion*. The proportional relationship of width and height of doors and windows within the District is generally one unit horizontal to two units vertical. New construction or renovations should conform to this standard.

   (v) *Signs*. Design and placement of signs on buildings should:
   - be limited as to the number and amount of information per building,
   - relate size to pedestrian scale,
   - relate proportion and location to complement the building's composition and architectural details,
   - consist of materials and be limited to colors which are appropriate to the facade design and materials,
   - use lettering styles, sizes and composition which relate to architectural style within the district,
   - be illuminated externally.[3]

119

Color

The question of compatibility in color is a tricky one; presumably, this sometimes refers to keeping everything white, as was apparently the original idea in Guildhall. In fact, particularly in northern Vermont, there is considerable variety in the color of buildings; in any event, Vermonters are likely to be prickly about being told how to paint their houses. It is, therefore, interesting (and rather surprising) that many of the ordinances do specifically authorize requirements for conformity in color, as in Winooski, Montpelier, and the three towns in the Northeast Kingdom.

Scope of Jurisdiction

Chapter 117 contains a clause spelling out specifically what types of changes are regulated in these districts: "No structure may be erected, reconstructed, substantially altered, restored, moved, demolished, or changed in use or type of occupancy" without special permission. This language is usually repeated verbatim in the ordinances. Montpelier has an important modification in connection with demolition—that no building of unique historic or architectural value may be demolished unless there is an affirmative showing that the building is incapable of earning "an economic return," whatever that might mean; the planning commission is instructed to consider the feasibility of "all other available alternatives."[4] The Winooski ordinance adds a reference to changes in color, materials, lighting, fencing, and walls.

Some ordinances contain various provisions limiting the scope of authority thereunder. For example, the Burlington ordinance indicates that it does not apply to ordinary small-scale maintenance and repair, nor for changes made in accordance with an order from a public official in order to protect safety. Several ordinances (as in Manchester) explicitly limit concern to exterior changes so that interior changes are not affected; the Winooski ordinance further limits concern to exterior changes that are in public view. Wilmington instructs those administering the ordinance not to insist on any one architectural style and indicates that conformity to the architectural details in a prevailing style should be regarded as merely a suggestion, and that this is not to be required in all instances. Burlington contains a clause that is quite familiar in historic preservation law, instructing the administrators to be strict in enforcing the requirements as to buildings with high architectural value but to be lenient in dealing with buildings of little historic value unless proposed changes in the latter would be detrimental to more important buildings in the surrounding area.

Types of Construction Regulated

As with historic preservation ordinances generally, most of the proceedings under these ordinances have to do with relatively minor construction projects—changes in windows and porches, other additions to houses or garages, sheds, siding, and signs. In the first year of experience in Woodstock, requests for bay window additions played a leading role. Burlington has been having an acute housing shortage, and so it is not surprising that many of the proceedings there have involved conversion of older houses to multiple-dwelling use.

Some of the ordinances contain specific provisions referring to signs. For example, the Burlington ordinance states that size, location, and various other features of signs must not detract from the surrounding area; the Winooski ordinance requires specifically that signs be compatible with the neighborhood in size, color, shape, and materials. There are also detailed provisions on the permitted size and height of various kinds of signs.

HOW THESE ORDINANCES ARE ADMINISTERED

In the fall of 1984, a special land use clinic at the Vermont Law School investigated the actual administration of design control ordinances in the eleven Vermont towns that have such ordinances. The most striking finding (although hardly a surprising one) is the great variety of experience in the administration of these ordinances. The towns with such ordinances vary widely in the type of control imposed, the attitude toward the idea of public regulation, the principal problems encountered, and the volume of business resulting. Nevertheless, certain common denominators come through clearly.

Basis of Success

Some of these programs have been generally recognized as quite successful, and the reasons for success are what one would expect. Where there is strong public support, that naturally leads to more effective administration; this has clearly played a role in Old Bennington, Manchester, and Woodstock. In some cases the talent available on the design review board is strikingly able and effective, as in Winooski and Woodstock. The general practice in the successful programs has involved a lot of negotiation between the public officials and the private developer, with the public officials feeling free to offer their own suggestions for possible modifications, sometimes to the applicant's advantage; this is particularly clear in Old Bennington, Winooski, and Woodstock. Where a detailed plan has been adopted and is used as a backup to make policy guidance more specific, as in Woodstock, Manchester, and Guildhall, this, of course, has been helpful. In one instance (Winooski), the design review arrangements were one part of an overall rehabilitation of an old factory town by urban renewal and shared in the public regard resulting from the success of those operations.

121

The Principal Problems

Some of the main problems encountered recur in several towns. In the most obvious example, in at least two towns (Montpelier and Greensboro), some or most of the officials in charge of administration and enforcement have at best limited enthusiasm for design control and not much belief in restraints on private property owners generally.[5] In that situation, naturally restrictions are often not enforced, variances are rife (officially granted or by inaction), and in one town, work was often started on alterations before design control approval was forthcoming. Moreover, in those situations where, in effect, no plan exists or where it is not used for effective backup, policy guidance is lacking, especially because in these instances the criteria in the ordinance are phrased in general terms. (For example, in Burlington, only one copy of the plan could be found; this hardly suggests that it is widely used.)

In Woodstock, Wilmington, and Guildhall, the criteria are quite specific and quite similar among the three; in other towns, they are phrased in general terms of "compatibility" and "harmony," and so wide discretion is left to the administrators. Not surprisingly, as in Burlington, this has led to widespread charges that decisions on design control are based purely on whim (or, conversely, "common sense"); the same is apparently true in Greensboro. Finally, in several towns, no adequate records are kept; at most, there is a record of the request and the decision made but no explanation of why. Obviously, in such situations, effective judicial review is severely inhibited and, at best, extraordinarily difficult; it is equally hard for interested observers to find out whether consistent lines of policy are or are not being followed, and, indeed, what they are.

Number of Applications

In several towns, the design control ordinances have generated substantial business. This is most strikingly so in Burlington, where the ordinance covers about half of the city and the applications have often run around one hundred per year. However, there are also substantial numbers of applications each year in Winooski, Montpelier, and Manchester. At the other extreme, in Guildhall, there has been only one proceeding over about a ten-year period, though both plan and ordinance are particularly interesting. Other towns have been relatively quiescent, as with about ten applications per year in Greensboro and less in Old Bennington.

In almost all these towns, the great majority of applications have resulted in the grant of permits. However, in the towns where the ordinance is more effective, the permits have been accompanied by a series of conditions; in a few instances, there have been flat turndowns. This is particularly true in Manchester, Old Bennington, Burlington, and Woodstock.

Policies Followed

In a few cases, the consideration of applications under design control ordinances has resulted in some interesting decisions on policy. In particular, situations have arisen where there is an obvious potential conflict between adhering to historic reality and conforming to current notions of aesthetics. In Manchester, a house that had been "modernized" in the Victorian period, so that the residents were quite used to its revised appearance, was sought to be restored to its original architecture; there was a good deal of resistance from people in the town. However, the Manchester authorities agreed to approve the restoration. In a similar incident in Woodstock, the purchaser of a house on the Green found what was obviously a rather heavy portico, which clearly belonged originally over the front door, and received permission to put it back there. No one would argue with enthusiasm that this was an aesthetic improvement.

In many towns, the work of the authorities in design review has been concentrated primarily on signs, which are, of course, an important part of the appearance of an area and one where a lot of harm could be done. This is particularly obvious in Winooski, where this is by far the most important problem and where the board has adopted a strong policy against any signs that include the logos of nationally advertised products. (Such signs are available free to the shop owner.) In Burlington, the stated primary policies are to protect lake views (which is obvious from the ordinance) and to protect the character of the established neighborhoods, which must involve a lot of judgment over so large an area. The board in Woodstock has concerned itself frequently with the question of permitting bay windows, to replace ordinary windows, and has flatly refused to approve vinyl siding in the following terms:

> We recommend denial of the application for installation of vinyl siding as we find no compelling reason for its use within the Historic District. It is an inappropriate material which would not enhance the appearance of the building, nor, in our opinion, function any better in conserving energy than thorough caulking and weatherstripping or retain a good appearance longer than a well applied paint job. Although the structure is not one of particular distinction, it harmonizes well with its neighbors in size and general design and we are unwilling to establish a precedent for what must be considered a downscaling of an historic area by the installation of an artificial material where the existing historic material exists in reasonably good condition needing only minor repair and paint. We appreciate the willingness of the contractor to respect all architectural trim features such as cornerboards, windows and door trim, etc., but we feel the nature of the vinyl material would require frequent and unacceptable compromise of those features.

> Although the new garage lies outside the Historic District, it is observable very clearly from the street. If the gable end faces the street we recommend that the pitch of the roof replicate that of the street facade of the house. We would prefer that the new structure be reoriented to present a shed-like appearance from the street. If it were designed with a short high steep roof in front and a long sloping one in the rear (typical salt box) snow would not present as much of a problem as with equal sized roofs.

Should the applicant wish to replace existing 2 over 2 sash with smaller more numerous panes such as 6 over 6—permission to do so is hereby granted so far as this Board may be concerned.[6]

The authorities in Old Bennington expressed considerable concern with the possibility of increased density, which would, of course, make a difference there, and over protection of their large trees.

Procedure

The most striking procedural lack under these ordinances is the failure to keep proper records, to make judicial review effective, and to satisfy anyone interested in whether there is consistent policy or not. Until recently, even the authorities in Woodstock had no such records; this is still true in Old Bennington, where all that is available is the record of the request and the decision made with nothing on the rationale. On the other hand, excellent records appear to be kept in Winooski. In Manchester, it is said that the records are informal.

In at least one instance (in Woodstock), the fourteen-day period allowed before a permit must be granted automatically is far too short and has resulted in a lot of permits granted in default of any decision. Moreover, the complaint is practically universal that enforcement is inadequate. The towns vary widely in procedures adopted to exempt certain minor improvements from the scope of the legislation.

RECOMMENDATIONS

Local administration is always the weakest element in American land use controls, and it is a pleasure to be able to report that some of those ordinances appear to be working well. Nevertheless, several recommendations for improvement are implicit in the analysis:

1. Fairly specific statements on policy are needed in the plan and/or ordinance to provide guidance to those administering the ordinance. There is no reason to be surprised, when legal standards are as vague as "harmony" and "compatibility," that these have resulted in complaints of inconsistency and unfairness. The examples quoted on more specific standards, from Woodstock and Wilmington, make it clear that there is no validity here to the argument often made that it is impossible to provide better standards.
2. Another serious weakness revealed in the survey—and the one easiest to correct—is the failure to keep proper records of such proceedings. Minutes should be kept of all meetings. Moreover, any decision (except the most trivial) should be accompanied by findings and a statement (in fairly specific terms) of why the proposed construction was approved or disapproved. Since

meetings on such matters often run to late at night, this is best handled by staff assistance.

3. Some effective enforcement mechanism is needed. The ordinance should provide for injunctive relief in important cases. Various lesser mechanisms are conceivable: for example, a requirement for filing photographs of the construction after its completion might solve a lot of problems.

Notes

1. 24 Vt. Stats. Ann. Sec. 4407(6).
2. Woodstock Village Zoning Ordinance, Sec. 4.104.
3. Wilmington Zoning Ordinance, Sec. C.
4. But see Note 5 below.
5. For example, the Montpelier Planning Commission apparently routinely approves all demolition requests with no great concern about the ordinance requirement about an "economic return."
6. Application V-682-84, George and Ann Baird, 15 River Street, April 1984.

A similar denial of a permit to install vinyl siding in a historic district was squarely upheld in *Anderson v. Old King's Highway Regional Historic Preservation Commission*, 397 Mass. 609, 493 N.E. 2d 188 (1986).

Chapter 8

Recommendations for the Future

THREE POSSIBLE MODELS

The basic decisions on a town's future are necessarily taken in the course of some sort of planning process.[1] What really counts is the spirit animating that process and, thus, its goals. Stated briefly, planning for the traditional Vermont towns could be aimed at any one of three quite different types of goals:

1. A museum town designed to exemplify the life of some past era, with primary emphasis on making houses available to visitors—and so a town with relatively little independent life of its own, on the model of Williamsburg or even Sturbridge Village.
2. A gentrified town, detached geographically from the metropolitan areas but with high-income in-migrants rapidly (or gradually) replacing the long established wide range of income groups among the town's residents—and with commercial facilities designed to cater either to the former or to the tourists.
3. A democratic town in the Vermont tradition, with a broad range of income groups living in an atmosphere of casual friendliness and with considerable social integration—and so a regard for the interests of different groups.

If market forces are left to dominate the scene, there is no question that in many towns there will be considerable progress toward gentrification. The market forces pushing toward gentrification are powerful, with new housing very expensive, with good existing housing priced at astronomical levels, with other widespread opportunities for capital gains both from open land and from commercial real estate,[2] and with many high-income people leaving the congested metropolitan areas and looking for a pleasant place to live. Whether any planning program can have an effective countervailing force is an open question; a planning program aimed at social and economic integration does have the advantage of following Vermont tradition but certainly will not have the benefit of coasting along with prevailing market forces. In this situation, a historic preservation program will probably not have any major effect, one way or the other, on the decision between gentrification and social integration.[3] Nevertheless, the question of its probable impact upon this choice must be squarely faced.

The recommendations herein for protecting and enhancing Vermont townscape reflect a definite choice in the direction of democratic social integration, and, thus, are squarely based on the assumption that planning in the democratic spirit is possible. The museum-town alternative is definitely rejected; on the contrary, emphasis is given to livening up civic activities in the center. The aesthetic component is, therefore, envisaged as merely one part of an overall planning approach, with due consideration for other objectives—and necessarily with a special concern for the needs of those less fortunate in the worldly sense.

In this context, difficult choices may sometimes be necessary, but there is no inherent contradiction between the different goals embraced. A program to preserve and to enhance the best of Vermont townscape will give some pleasure to all groups; older Vermonters may not be in the forefront of preservation action, but they are not insensitive to such matters.

Since most towns have a greater or less area of nonprime townscape, there is usually no need to invade prime townscape to find sites for less attractive uses. A fast-food restaurant may be needed somewhere, and perhaps a couple of competing filling stations, but no serious argument can be made that these must be in the middle of Newfane common.

RECOMMENDATIONS

As a result of the analysis in this report, the primary objectives for protecting and enhancing Vermont townscape, and the legal tools appropriate in each instance, can be spelled out as indicated below.

1. *To preserve the mountain vistas as the backdrop for most of the towns, by (a) keeping these slopes open and without buildings and (b) not blocking views of the slopes.* To keep open and without buildings, i.e., in woods or open fields, the slopes that dominate the towns are one of the most important aspects of Vermont townscape preservation. Where (as often) the slopes are steep, development pressure is not likely to be intense in any event; but this is not a place to take chances. In an extreme case, if there is any real danger of development, the slopes in question could be acquired publicly and maintained as a public park. In fact, that is exactly what has happened in some instances, as in Woodstock, where Mt. Tom (dominating the town from the north) is now a park (or rather two, as a result of two generous donations); Mt. Peg (to the southeast) is also partly in public ownership. That, however, is only the exceptional situation; lesser steps will normally be appropriate.

If the town is zoned, such slopes must necessarily be zoned in some district; this should, of course, be in a district that does not encourage development, especially commercial development or condominiums. A forest zone will often be appropriate.[4]

However, in many instances, the most effective technique in this respect is likely to be less-than-fee ownership, with the development rights acquired by the public. (In the first instance, it might be easier to acquire these for a period of years and secure the permanent rights later.) A good example of this would be the attractive wooded hillsides that loom up at both ends of the main street in Stowe. In addition, if an area is wooded, it may qualify for the new Vermont scheme providing tax concessions for good forestry management;[5] the town authorities should look into this possibility and discuss it with the owner.

To prevent a tall building blocking the views of such a slope is simple enough. All that is needed are the normal zoning height (and yard) restrictions in the right places.

2. *To preserve the vistas between buildings, with a field leading up to the forest edge.* The great majority of these Vermont towns are single-street towns. There is no other street parallel to the main street, and so the views in depth past the buildings along the main street are not blocked by the rear of buildings along such a parallel street. The important thing here is then a matter of street planning—to avoid laying out such a street.[6]

The remainder of this problem can be dealt with rather simply. Zoning regulations on side yards normally will, and in any event easily can, prevent a situation where existing views between buildings are blocked.[7] It is not necessarily a good idea to zone such streets for single-family detached housing, for that might block a desirable conversion of a large house into apartments. However, if new attached housing is permitted, there should be a strict limit on the maximum dimension of buildings parallel to the main street.

3. *To strengthen the focal point.* Major effort should be directed to enhancing and reinforcing the focal point (or points) of the town. Any proposed physical changes in the vicinity should be reviewed carefully in the light of these considerations. Major urban design expertise will often be appropriate in these situations.

4. *To preserve the integrity and quality of the town green and to increase its civic role in the town's life.* Where maintenance is inadequate to preserve the quality of town commons, an active citizens' group is needed to take the responsibility for this work—for mowing and fertilizing the grass, trimming shrubs, taking care of trees and benches, etc. The same group will need to restrict the erection of monuments, and especially to be on their guard against the increasing clutter of signs and inappropriate street lighting. Any attempt to invade the common for highway or parking purposes should be resisted vigorously.[8]

In this context, serious thought should be given to the possibilities for increasing the civic role of the town common, as part of an overall program for stimulating a livelier outdoor life in town. This will involve consideration of the changing role of outdoor activity in modern life in the North.

5. *To keep intact the concentration of institutional buildings at a central focal point.* There may be pressure in some towns to move a major public or private function now lodged in an existing institutional building to a new site outside town or at its edge, perhaps in order to obtain more room for parking or to save heating and maintenance costs in an older building, or perhaps merely because an ambitious developer would like to reinforce his shopping area away from the center.

Every effort should be made to prevent the removal of any important public and private buildings (except possibly schools) and functions or activity from the central area, particularly around a central common. If this should occur, the result will be a serious loss for the focal point in that particular town. Obviously, the demolition of such a building would be an even more serious loss. Possible adaptive reuses should be explored, along with the possibilities for federal tax relief in connection therewith.

To the extent that public buildings are involved in proposed demolitions, they need to be dealt with in the capital budget, or whatever passes for the same. In the case of private institutions, persuasion and historic districting would probably be the principal weapons available, together with civic pressure combined with a refusal to relax relevant regulations in order to facilitate such removal.

In those instances where the focal point is commercial (in whole or in part), the same principle applies. This will normally involve opposition to the development of peripheral shopping centers in these towns.

6. *To maintain the human scale by preventing the erection of buildings noticeably larger than the ordinary house.* Here again, the problem is relatively simple. Zoning height restrictions will prevent overly tall buildings; it is easy enough to insert in a zoning ordinance a prohibition of buildings that are longer than a certain dimension parallel to the street. An exception to these restrictions might occasionally be needed for a new church or institutional building of some dignity.

7. *To protect the appearance of historic districts.* The central areas in many of these towns are appropriate for protection by historic district regulations to preserve the existing facades, to prevent ugly new buildings, to restrict signs, and generally to avoid any kind of strikingly incompatible architecture. Indeed, nothing else will have any real effect.[9] Moreover, in a number of towns, it is clear that commercial establishments fit in much better if they are located in converted residential buildings than if they are

in new commercial buildings. The first legal basis for historic district ordinances in Vermont was found in the design control provisions of the Vermont zoning and planning enabling act. To date, only a few of the towns analyzed herein have such protection—Old Bennington, Guildhall, Manchester, and Woodstock.

Successful and evenhanded administration of historic district laws depends upon the existence of some fairly specific standards on what is meant by conformity to the existing historic character, both to provide substantive guidance to the administrators and to provide protection against legal attack. In a city with a unique kind of architecture (as in Santa Fe, New Mexico), there is no serious problem: the standards are provided by the distinctive and observable characteristics of the existing buildings.

The problem is not so easy in Vermont towns, whose townscape normally includes a variety of architectural styles although with certain repetitive common elements. The problem is to identify those common elements. The thirty towns include enough diversity so that there is no realistic possibility of drawing up a model ordinance on this point.

8. *To designate historic landmarks and provide for their protection.* Most of the towns involved in this study contain substantial areas of historic significance; but occasionally, there is a single building that has some similar significance but is not surrounded by others of the same character. In this situation, designation as a historic landmark is appropriate, with restrictions similar to those involved in historic districts. This was not provided for in Vermont law until the passage in 1986 of the historic districts provisions of the townscape bill, discussed below.

9. *To reduce clutter.* A lot can be done at the small scale to reduce clutter. One major opportunity here will be to work with the state Department of Transportation to reduce the frequently large number of duplicating directional signs. In other instances, good urban design will suggest rearrangement of monuments (or perhaps even the removal of some).

10. *To provide bypasses wherever needed to keep out heavy through traffic.* As indicated above, most of these towns are small and located in relatively remote places away from heavy traffic; several others have their own bypasses. However, this is a severe problem in a few of the towns, and there is no solution short of a bypass. For many years, there has been talk of an alternate route around the two towns most severely affected, Stowe and Woodstock.

11. *To restrict commercial strips at the main entrance to the larger towns.* Probably the most serious damage to pleasant Vermont towns has been the development of

messy commercial strips at the main entrance to town, particularly in the larger towns. The solution is relatively clear-cut and requires a state statute. At such locations, when commercial development is permitted, a narrow planting strip (5 feet to 10 feet deep) should be required (and maintained) between the highway and the commercial establishments;[10] some restrictions on highway access (by curb cuts or otherwise) and on signs will probably be appropriate.

12. *A local citizens' committee to promote good townscape.* During many discussions with residents of these towns in the course of preparation of this report, it became clear that Vermonters have a lot of lively interest in the problems discussed herein; this is particularly true in many of the towns here studied. In towns where concerned citizens have such an interest, they should be encouraged to form a committee to promote townscape protection and enhancement. In the larger towns (and some of the smaller ones), it would be desirable to retain professionally trained urban design experts for this purpose. The amount of money needed for this purpose is not large, and may be available either by local subscription or from interested foundations.

13. *Statutory implementation.* With a few important exceptions (primarily on ragged commercial strips along highways at the edge of the town), it is clear existing statutes give Vermont towns authority to make some use of most of the legal devices needed to implement the proposed program. However, with aesthetic regulations, it is particularly important to have statutory authority as explicit as possible. It is not entirely clear that the pre-existing statutes authorizing the use of specific devices (e.g., side yards) would include their use as a means of protecting vistas in townscape. Explicit statutory authority has been needed for use of the various devices, in addition to statutes covering the three areas mentioned above.

Such statutory authority will be useful primarily to provide an answer to legal challenges brought by developers who argue that statutory authority is lacking. Such a statement may also impose an affirmative duty upon towns to protect scenic townscape and so provide a legal weapon for protesting neighbors who feel that a town has been remiss in this respect.

A draft statute was introduced in 1985 as Vermont Senate Bill 69 to give the necessary authority to protect scenic townscape, and a somewhat modified version was enacted in 1986.[11] The bill was introduced by Senator (former Governor) Philip Hoff of Chittenden County, and Senator Harvey Carter of Bennington County. It was shepherded through the Legislature by the appropriate committee chairmen, Senator Arthur Gibb of Addison County and Representative Stephen Reynes of Pomfret.

The provisions lay a groundwork of recognition of the economic and social aspects of beautiful townscape, define the special characteristics of beauty in the towns, recognize and identify the primary threats to townscape, and provide explicit authority for the state and municipalities to protect scenic attributes of townscape.

Section 2 of the law provides specific legislative findings of fact, along the lines set forth in this report. These findings are used to establish a clear legislative intent to protect particular aesthetic attributes because of their historical, economic, scenic, and cultural importance. These findings are as follows:

(1) The state of Vermont possesses a natural and human-made environment which is widely recognized as one of the most attractive anywhere in the world. A distinctive and most valuable aspect of this environment is any harmonious combination of natural features and human settlements.

(2) Among the state's varied historic and scenic resources, are towns which still resemble in some important respects the earliest permanent settlements. The special characteristics of these towns include the following:

(A) A concentrated urban settlement with striking vistas all around.

(B) A linear pattern of development, usually along a single street (but often widening briefly at the green), so that views between buildings usually extend across open fields and up to the forest edge.

(C) A central focal point which serves to give the town a characteristic image and a sense of its identity. This focal point is usually at (or near) a centrally-located town green.

(D) The buildings in this central area are predominantly 1½ to 2½ stories and the area may contain a few buildings with special dignity, such as a church and courthouse.

(E) The architecture is of unusually high quality with a wide variety of architectural styles, including most of those characteristic of the early 19th century. Other amenities are often present—including tall trees, a limited amount of commercial activity around the green, and the absence of heavy traffic.

(3) The state's historic and scenic resources have contributed greatly to its economic development, by encouraging native Vermonters to remain in the state and by attracting visitors, new industries, and new cultural facilities; and such resources thus help to support existing and new businesses and recreational establishments, to encourage new investment, to increase employment and real income in the state, and to support the tax structure of the state and its local subdivisions. The state's historic and scenic resources are threatened by new development which is inappropriately placed and incompatible with

132

such resources, by changes in the patterns of retailing and providing services, and by decentralization of both commercial and community facilities. Moreover, some of the most attractive towns in the state are often choked by heavy traffic.

Section 3, Legislative Statement of Purpose, states that it is the policy of the state of Vermont to preserve and enhance its historic and scenic resources. This section strengthens the law by stating that Vermont's historic and scenic townscape resources are of the essence and, therefore, "should be given special protection and enhanced wherever possible."

The existing provisions authorizing design control districts (set forth at the start of Chapter 7) were amended to include good townscape. Referring to the areas covered:

> Such areas may include townscape areas which resemble in important aspects the earliest permanent settlements, including a concentrated urban settlement with striking vistas, views extending across open fields and up to the forest edge, a central focal point and town green, and buildings of high architectural quality including styles of the early nineteenth century.

Moreover, in the course of legislative passage, the bill was (very sensibly) combined with new and improved provisions specifically dealing with "historic districts," as contrasted with "design control districts," and spelling out how they are to be administered, as well as new provisions on landmarks. New provisions on the transfer of development rights were also included in the same law.

Notes

1. Whether or not so labeled, and regardless of how well thought through the process is.
2. A recent incident in one of the towns is not reassuring. A principal building downtown was bought by relative newcomers to town, and the commercial rents were promptly *quintupled*. The natural result of this sort of action is a highly unstable pattern of high-priced specialized retailing, not catering to local residents at all, i.e., innumerable "gifte shoppes."
3. On the other hand, one may predict with confidence that it will automatically be blamed for whatever may happen that someone doesn't like.
4. As specifically authorized in the state planning act, 24 Vt. Stats. Ann. Sec. 4407(1)(B).
5. 32 Vt. Stats. Ann. Ch. 124, Sec. 3751 *et seq*.
6. It must be recognized that if a town is really growing, such a policy may (and often necessarily will) encourage an elongated pattern of ribbon development, which may not be very desirable either. Some difficult choices may be required here. If a parallel street is, in fact, really necessary, careful and sensitive site planning may help solve the resulting problem.
7. It is assumed here that the views in question are not so broad as to destroy another value, a sense of enclosure.

8. An excellent detailed program for improving town greens and making better use of them is set forth in R. L. Fleming and L. A. Halderman, *On Common Ground* (1982). Emphasis is given to landscaping, footpaths, and furnishings, as well as to reinforcing the focal points.

9. Restrictions on what color a house may be painted are likely to be severely resisted and, in any event, would be appropriate only in the unusual case when practically all the buildings in a town are a single color (as white-with-green-shutters in Newfane). It would be useful, however, to have a procedure for enforced delay and an opportunity to try persuasion if repainting is proposed in some outlandish color, as in the well-known incident when a block front in the New Orleans Vieux Carre was painted lavender.

10. To draft such a statute, it will be necessary to resolve some fairly complex problems: first of all, to delimit and define the areas where it is to apply, and then to deal with problems, such as the frequency and the width of curb cuts and driveways, adequate sight distances, what trees and shrubs are desirable in this context, possible conflicts between trees and public utilities, etc. See, for example, American Society of Planning Officials, *Planning Advisory Service*, No. 86 (1956), No. 177 (1963), and No. 293 (1973).

11. Vermont Laws 1986, Chapter 243.

Chapter 9

Selected Town Plans
With Commentary by Professor Wilhelm V. von Moltke*

By definition, the towns covered in this report retain much of their historic quality. However, in many instances, these towns have suffered some minor damage in various ways, including such matters as trees missing, overhead wires, and excessive paving with blacktop. Definite opportunities exist for enhancing even the best townscape. Plans for such improvements in five towns, selected to indicate a variety of conditions, illustrate the possibilities here.

A group of illustrative site plans of commons are described to show the potential for rehabilitation and enhancement of these focal areas. The following commons are included:

• Chelsea • Strafford • Randolph Center • Stowe • South Royalton

CHELSEA

Existing development on the periphery of both commons is quite dense with the following exceptions where additional buildings would be appropriate: (1) the eastern corner of the southern edge of the North Common; (2) the western edge of the road across from the area between the commons; and (3) the western portion of the southern limit of the South Common. In the second instance, this would require a new location for the existing playground and may not be desirable.

The North Common provides the setting for a number of public buildings, which include the United Church, the town hall and town library, and the general store. The South Common provides the setting for the courthouse and for a regional school.

Both commons are surrounded by almost complete lines of peripheral trees. The North Common has six gaps and the South Common has two trees missing. The illustrative site plan shows continuous street trees on both sides of the surrounding street and along the main north and south street for a distance of about two hundred fifty feet.

* Wilhelm V. von Moltke, FAIA, AICP, is Professor of Urban Design, Emeritus, at the Harvard Graduate School of Design.

135

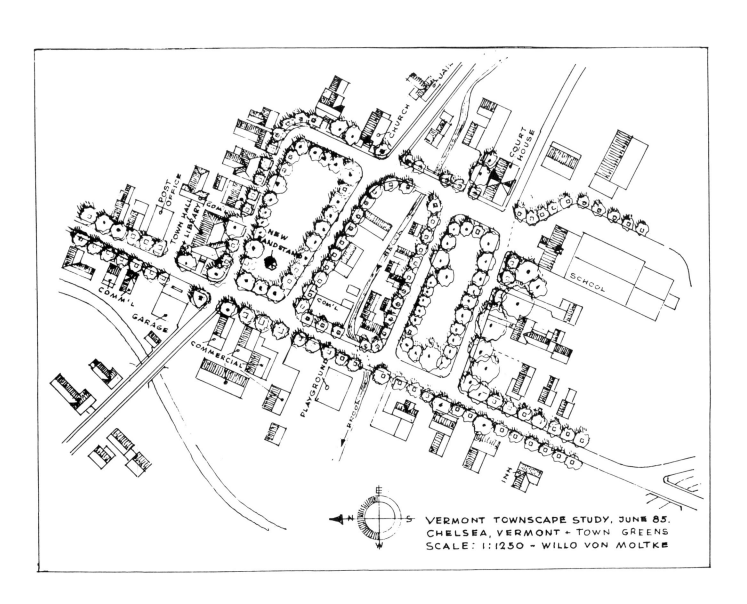

VERMONT TOWNSCAPE STUDY, JUNE 85.
CHELSEA, VERMONT + TOWN GREENS
SCALE: 1:1250 - WILLO VON MOLTKE

Both commons suffer from unsightly overhead wires, inappropriate street lighting, unsightly traffic and street signs, and excessive blacktop paving.

The illustrative site plan incorporates the following recommendations:

1. Replace the missing trees surrounding the commons.
2. Supplement existing and plant new trees on both sides of streets surrounding both commons, and also along the main street that provides the access to both commons for the distance shown on the illustrative plan. Trees are identified as follows:

existing trees   proposed new trees

3. Bury all cables within this area.
4. Provide street lighting in harmony and scale with the historic buildings in this central area.
5. Replace street and traffic signs with signs that are in harmony with the historic buildings in the area.
6. Reduce blacktop paving to two twelve-foot-wide lanes, provide parking lanes paved with gravel or Belgian blocks, and change the areas that have been gained as park into lawn. Furthermore, pave the sidewalks with bricks and widen these at street corners, thus eliminating parking at these points and making it easier for pedestrians to cross the street. Eliminate parking on the periphery of the two commons. When the demand for parking warrants, 45° parking can be used instead of curb parking along the sidewalks.

These guidelines, which must be supplemented with rules regarding floor area ratio, spacing, position on the lot, volume, height, and architectural character of new buildings, should assure appropriate rehabilitation and enhancement of the Chelsea commons.

STRAFFORD

The Strafford Common was deeded to the town in 1802 and evolved to its present shape in 1906. The quality of this open space is reinforced by the similarity of building scale, style, materials, spacing, and orientation to the access roads. This character

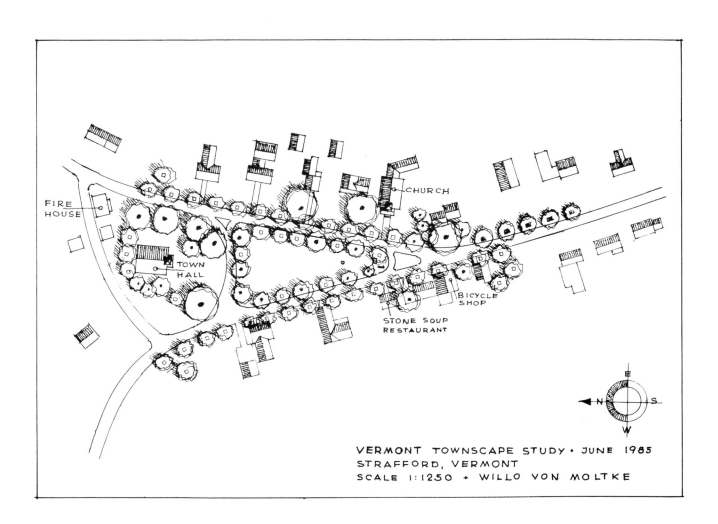

FIRE HOUSE

TOWN HALL

CHURCH

BICYCLE SHOP

STONE SOUP RESTAURANT

VERMONT TOWNSCAPE STUDY • JUNE 1985
STRAFFORD, VERMONT
SCALE 1:1250 + WILLO VON MOLTKE

is enhanced by the Town House, which was built in 1799 on the northern hill over-looking the present common. This is a dramatic climax for the harmonious composition of the Strafford Common.

The appearance of this common can be enhanced by (1) supplementing the trees lining the edge of the common and both sides of the approach road, as shown on the illustrative site plan. Trees are indicated as follows:

existing trees   proposed new trees

(2) by burying all cables, and (3) by reducing the area paved with blacktop to two twelve-foot-wide traffic lanes and parallel eight-foot-wide parking lanes covered with gravel.

RANDOLPH CENTER

Apart from the "original common," Randolph Center has a unique urban design element of a landscaping nature—that is, a double row of trees on both sides of a modest pedestrian path forming a magnificent dense avenue. This element extends from the original common north along Main Street to the post office and general store.

The illustrative site plan shows the avenue of trees parallel to, and east of, Main Street, as well as a double row of trees defining the limits of the original common at the southern end of the avenue of trees. Such a spatial element would bring to life again a piece of the history of Randolph Center and provide a space enclosed by trees for special events during the summer months.

In addition, it is proposed to develop a walkway at the center of the avenue of trees following Main Street, with benches near the northern end not far from the general store, at the Congregational Church, and at the elementary school. Furthermore, it is proposed to place all cables underground and to develop appropriate street lighting for the pedestrian avenue for the illumination of Main Street.

These guidelines must be supplemented with rules regarding allowable floor area ratios, spacing, position on the lot, volume, height, and the architectural character of new buildings.

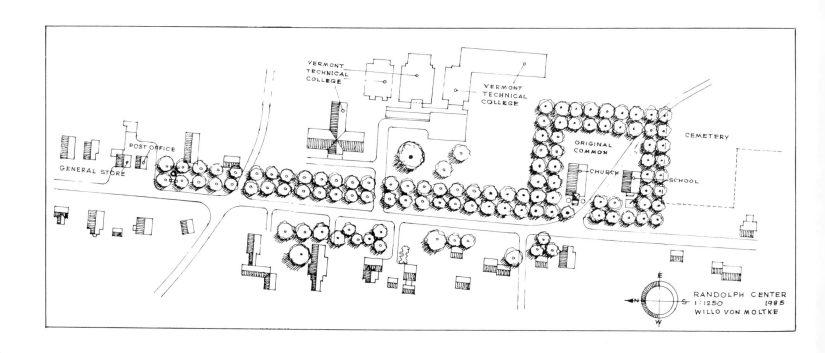

VERMONT
TECHNICAL
COLLEGE

VERMONT
TECHNICAL
COLLEGE

CEMETERY

ORIGINAL
COMMON

POST OFFICE

GENERAL STORE

CHURCH

SCHOOL

RANDOLPH CENTER
1:1250   1985
WILLO VON MOLTKE

STOWE

Stowe is unusual amongst these Vermont towns since it has no common.

The illustrative site plan shows that one can develop a system of tree-shaded sidewalks that connect the most important public buildings. The proposed network connects the inn, the "Soldier's Memorial," the church, the post office, and the municipal library adjacent to the elementary school.

This plan should be linked to other improvements, such as the paving of sidewalks in brick (including crossings) and the widening of the sidewalks at the intersections, to eliminate parking near the corners and to make the crossing of roads easier for the pedestrian. Improvements should also include the paving of the parking areas with gravel or Belgian blocks, the burying of all overhead wires, the improvement of street lighting in scale with the prevailing architecture, the provision of street furniture, and the improvement of street and traffic signs throughout the central area of Stowe.

SOUTH ROYALTON

The central open space of South Royalton was first restricted to be used as a park in 1868 when it was sold by Paul Dillingham to George Tarbell. In 1881, the land was sold to a group of Royalton citizens with the intention to allow the transfer of the park to the village of South Royalton upon incorporation. Since 1935, this park or common has been maintained by the Royalton Fire District and used by the town of Royalton.

The park is well defined in the west by a continuous row of retail stores with residential and service uses above and in the east and north by more open development, which is predominantly residential and includes a church and an inn. In the south, there is presently a post office, plus a bank and Senior Citizens' facility in the old railroad station bordering the tracks. The eastern end of the narrow strip between the street and the railroad track is still undeveloped. Some development would be desirable in this strip to complete the sense of enclosure around the green, with open space between buildings to permit the pleasant view of the rapidly rising landscape to the south of the railroad tracks.

The park contains a good number of substantial trees, which are also present on the other side of the adjacent streets to the east and to the south. The park itself is well used by the citizens of South Royalton. During the summer and fall, there are regular concerts in the bandstand by the town band; frisbee games and practice prevail during the spring, summer, and fall; there are occasional flea markets and church sales; the four-day Old Home Days celebration in July; as well as graduation ceremonies for the high school and Vermont Law School.

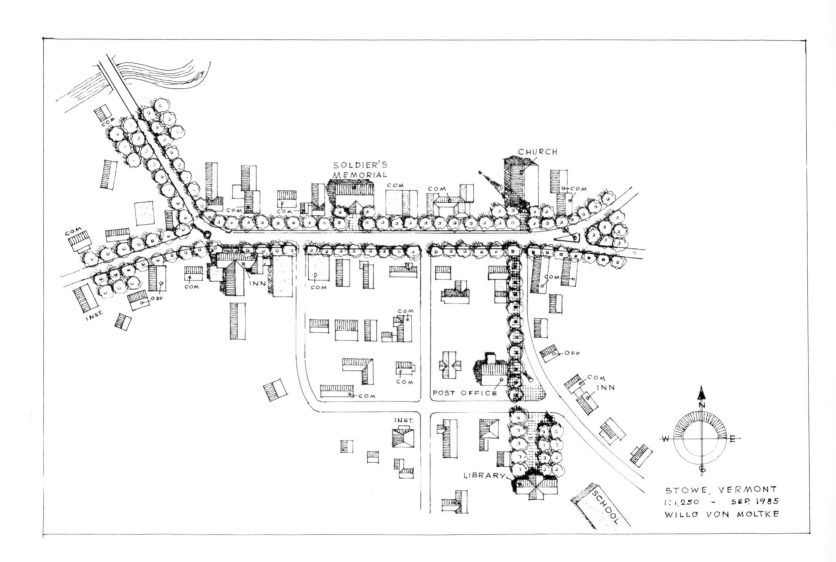

SOLDIER'S MEMORIAL

CHURCH

COM

COM

COM

COM

COM

INN

COM

OFF

INST.

COM

COM

COM

COM

OFF

COM INN

POST OFFICE

INST.

LIBRARY

SCHOOL

STOWE, VERMONT
1:1,250 - SEP. 1985
WILLO VON MOLTKE

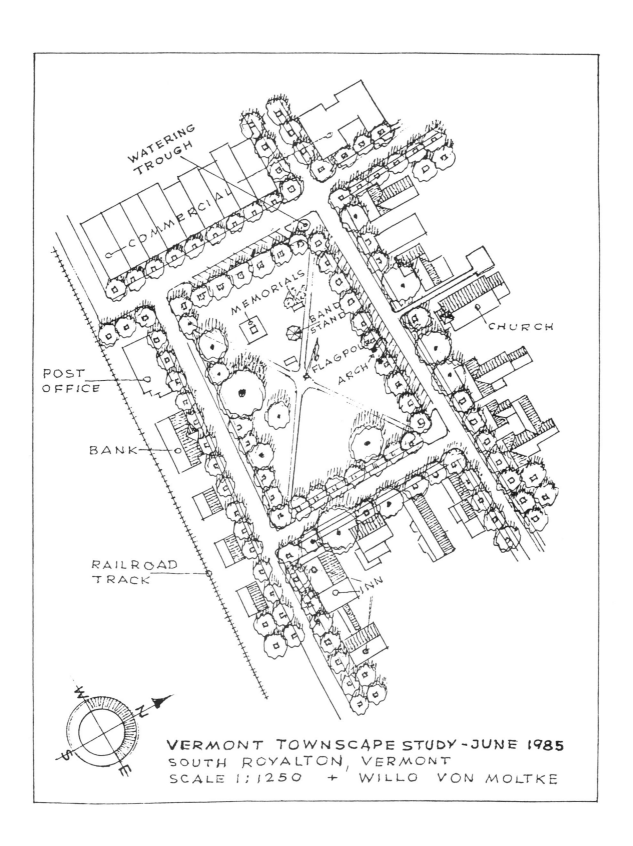

WATERING
TROUGH

COMMERCIAL

MEMORIALS

BAND
STAND

CHURCH

FLAGPOLE

ARCH

POST
OFFICE

BANK

RAILROAD
TRACK

INN

VERMONT TOWNSCAPE STUDY - JUNE 1985
SOUTH ROYALTON, VERMONT
SCALE 1:1250   + WILLO VON MOLTKE

The illustrative site plan shows a number of changes that, in the author's opinion, will enhance the quality of this park. These long-term design objectives include:

1. Reduction of the paved area (in particular in front of the retail row) that, according to the survey, is eighty feet wide. Fifty feet should suffice to accommodate one lane of curb parking (in front of the retail row), two traffic lanes, and one 45° parking lane adjacent to the park. This would provide a widened sidewalk to permit the planting of trees and parking for twenty-eight cars in the street. The northern boundary street of the park is shown with basically the same spatial organization. Here, forty cars can be parked. Curb parking has been provided in the eastern and southern boundary streets, resulting in forty-eight parking spaces. The total adds up to 116 spaces.

2. It is also proposed to use blacktop paving only for the traffic lanes and to pave the parking areas with Belgian blocks or to finish these with gravel. The sidewalks should be paved with bricks, which should also be used for pedestrian crossings.

3. Furthermore, it is recommended to eliminate the wirescape and to bury all cables in the area of the park.

4. The illustrative site plan shows also the character of the proposed tree planting:

existing trees   proposed new trees

It is proposed to frame the park or common with a single row of trees; the adjacent streets and their extensions should also be lined by trees, as shown on the illustrative site plan.

5. The street lighting should be efficient, not blinding, and in character with the park.

6. Street, storefront, and traffic signs should be harmonious with the character of the environment.

7. The much discussed watering trough northeast of the South Royalton Common has been incorporated into the landscaped area of the common, thus eliminating the hazardous aspect of this historical element.

Needless to say, the plans for each of the towns are long-term goals and may not be attained for thirty or forty years. They provide starting points, however, for local discussion of preservation and enhancement of the towns. Improvements in these towns could, in turn, provide incentives for other villages and towns to undertake similar projects.

APPENDICES

The oldest house in Royalton: Cape Cod Colonial

Appendix A

The Predominant Architectural Styles in Vermont Towns Prior to World War I

COLONIAL—CAPE COD, 1½ STORIES

1. Central chimney (occasionally supplanted later by two small "stove" chimneys).

2. Front door in center of long side facing street.

3. One row of small glass panes at top of front door. No glass at sides of door. (Front door frequently changed later to add Greek Revival "side" windows.)

4. Windows on facade high, usually directly under roof edge. Early windows tend to be longer and narrower than later windows. Originally 12 over 12 panes (frequently replaced with Victorian 2 over 2, thus destroying scale and design).

5. Small eaves, or merely a molding. (This frequently altered later as broad eaves were added.)

6. Clapboard construction (usually).

7. In Vermont, at gable ends on second floor, frequently small "eaves" windows, as in this illustration:

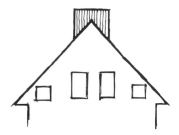

Note: This is an architectural detail less frequently seen outside Vermont.

Butternut Inn, Royalton: Georgian style

GEORGIAN

1. Two-and-one-half stories.

2. Although building is not square, the difference between width and length is less than in other styles. Thus, a "heavier" look is created.

3. Formal and symmetrical.

4. Pediments over front door, which is at center of long side facing street. Architectural detail is bold and projecting.

5. Central bay of front facade given special prominence, sometimes with carving, leading to central hallway from front to back of house.

6. Gable-ended roofs (usually).

7. Chimneys symmetrical either at ends or halfway between ends and center.

8. In Vermont, usually wood; elsewhere, frequently brick.

9. Likely to have substantial portico at front door, perhaps a later addition.

149

Foxstand Inn, Royalton: Federal style with parapet gable end

Dennison House, Royalton: Federal style

FEDERAL—USUALLY 2½ STORIES

1. Front door in center of long side.

2. Much glass around front door and down sides; often semicircular (fan-shaped) window above front door.

3. Wooden fan above front door of farmhouses with low ceilings.

4. Often hip roof with chimneys at short sides of house.

5. Palladian windows frequent in center of second floor.

6. Second-story windows well below carved eaves; frequent use of carved, ornate lintels.

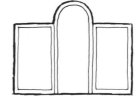

7. Much detail in trim; Egg & Dart; Tryglyphs & Metopes; pilasters, fine and light in appearance.

8. Clapboard or brick.

9. Originally 12-over-12 windows often altered to 6-over-6 or 2-over-2, which changes the pattern of the facade.

10. Often gabled porch supported by two columns protecting the front entrance door or a flat-roofed portico surmounted with a small balustrade.

11. In Vermont, there are frequently parapet gables.

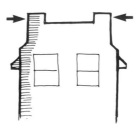

Community Church, Royalton: Greek Revival showing transition to Gothic Revival on steeple

KEVIN EATON

Tuller House, Royalton: Greek Revival

KEVIN EATON

GREEK REVIVAL

1. Use of white columns.

2. Gable roof with short side usually facing street.

3. Front door normally at one side of front facade, not in middle. Frequently with flat-roofed pillared portico.

4. Carving of trim is simple and based on Greek designs, angular and flat.

5. Stress on heavy triangular pediment at gable ends (A). If lower element of pediment is absent then heavy return of eaves (B).

 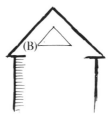

6. Six-over-six windows sometimes changed to 2-over-2 (but infrequently, as compared to Federal and Georgian structures).

Sylvia House, South Royalton: Gothic Revival

Morrill House, Strafford: Gothic Revival

GOTHIC REVIVAL

1. Gothic arches whenever possible.

2. Very high peaked gables.

3. Often "board and batten" wall.

4. Heavy carved "barge boards"(A).

5. Recessed balconies (B). This is a feature rarely seen outside Vermont. It also occurs in buildings of a style transitional between Greek Revival and Gothic Revival.

6. Frequent porches with roof supports carved with Gothic detail.

7. Sculptured chimneys.

8. Six-over-six windows.

Store, South Royalton: Italianate

ITALIANATE

1. Flat or flattish roofs.

2. Building is basically square and often has a square tower.

3. Very heavy projecting eaves supported by heavy carved brackets often in pairs. Often quoins at corners.

4. Heavy and carved trim, e.g., on window and door lintels.

5. Heavy and often "sculptured" chimneys.

6. Many porches.

7. Plan rarely symmetrical.

8. Everything, including interior rooms, overscale. Gives appearance of having been built for giants.

Woodstock: French Second Empire

FRENCH SECOND EMPIRE

1. Mansard roofs (A).

2. Dormer windows with heavy carved trim.

3. Sometimes quoins or pilasters at corners (B).

4. Resembles Italianate and occasionally has a square tower.

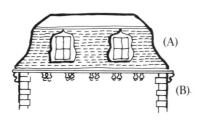

Norman Williams Public Library, Woodstock: Richardson Romanesque

RICHARDSON ROMANESQUE

1. Usually stone or brick or mixed stone and brick. Stone often roughly hewn or "rock-faced."

2. Windows and doors with round arches.

3. Often French "pepper pot" turrets.

4. Heavily "sculptured" chimneys.

5. Horizontal stress, use of heavy string courses.

6. Corbelled eaves.

7. Use of terra cotta sculptured decoration.

8. Rarely used for residential building in Vermont.

9. Metal or slate roofs.

Abbott House, Vermont Law School, South Royalton: Queen Anne style

QUEEN ANNE

1. Multiplicity of materials and details; e.g., clapboards, flush boards, shingles in many shapes, stones and brick (usually several kinds used in one building).

2. Towers, turrets, oriel windows, bay windows.

3. Porches.

4. Complex wood spindles and balustrades.

5. Sometimes chimneys appear and disappear behind eaves.

Herdsman's Cottage, Billings Farm, Woodstock: Stick style

STICK STYLE

1. Like Queen Anne but stress on "half-timbered" look of Elizabethan England.

2. Eastlake detail on porch fronts, balusters, etc.

Inn, Wilmington: Shingle style

SHINGLE STYLE

1. Less elaborate than Queen Anne. Plain shingles used on most of exterior walls instead of clapboard.

2. Low "swooping" lines, a streamlined effect.

3. Infrequent in Vermont.

Munson House, South Royalton: Prairie style

PRAIRIE OR BUNGALOW STYLE

1. Stress on low horizontal look.

2. Japanese influence (e.g., ends of beams are stressed on exterior).

3. Often clapboard or shingles.

4. Very heavy eaves.

5. Frank Lloyd Wright influence.

6. Often porches with heavy posts supporting roofs.

7. Infrequent in Vermont.

SPECIAL VERMONT ARCHITECTURAL DETAILS

Although the following architectural characteristics are found in other states, the following four appear to be especially frequent in Vermont:

1. The "lazy" window (see (A) below).

2. The small "eaves" windows in Colonial–Cape Cod houses (see p. 147)

3. Recessed balconies, cut *into* the gable ends of Gothic Revival houses, instead of protruding from them (see p. 155).

4. Parapet gable ends on Federal style brick houses (see p. 151).

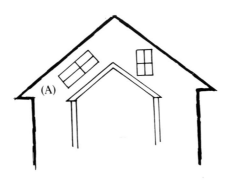

Appendix B

The Pattern of Buildings in the Central Areas

As indicated in Chapter 4, the pattern of buildings in the central parts of Vermont towns—usually around the Green—is a prime feature in Vermont townscape. While certain standard elements recur—the white clapboard church, an inn, maybe a courthouse, some residences, etc.—there is a good deal of variety and detail. To illustrate this, the following series of diagrams show in detail the existing use of such areas in eleven towns. A similar map of Brandon is found on pages 100 and 101.

LEGEND:

 GREEN

INN	INN
CH	Church
S	School
L	Library
PO	Post Office
TH	Town Hall
HS	Historical Society
CT	Courthouse
F	Firehouse

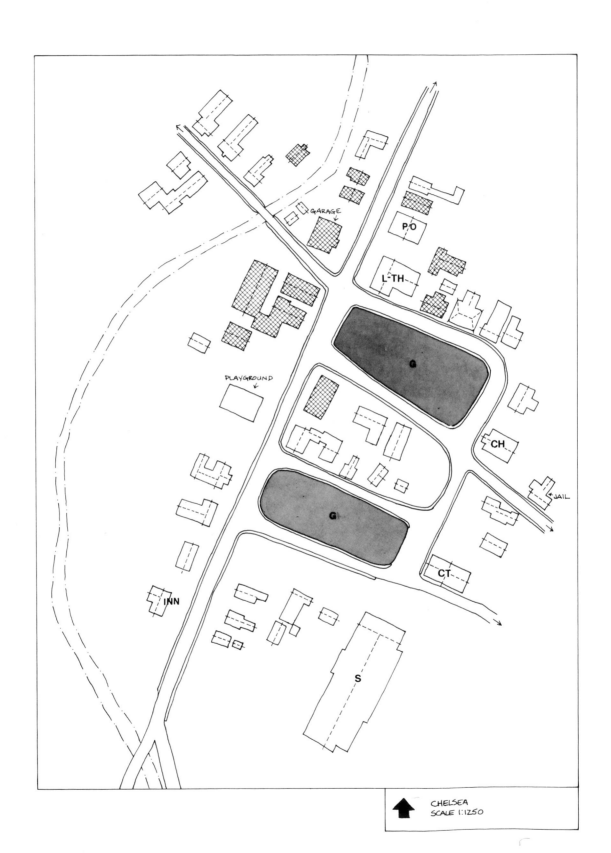

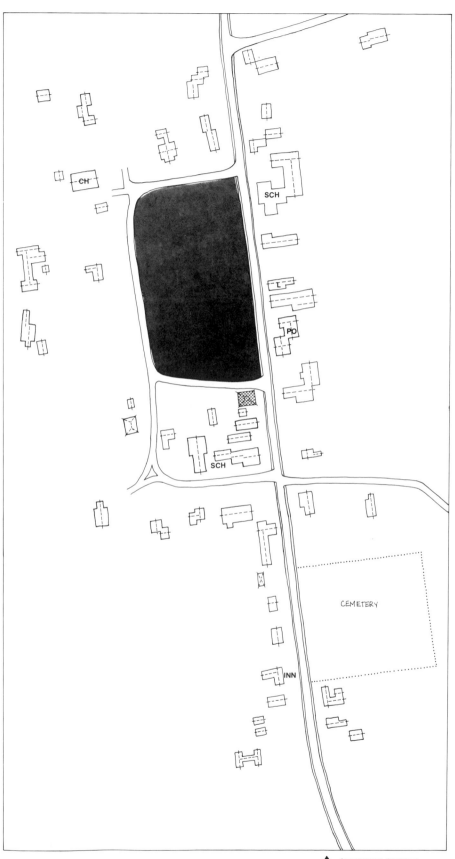

CH

SCH

T

PO

SCH

CEMETERY

INN

CRAFTSBURY COMMON
1:1250

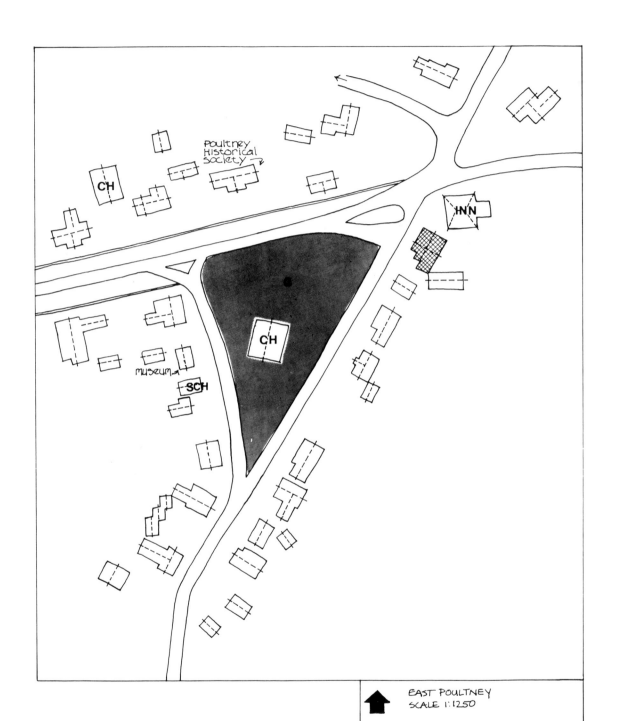

Poultney
Historical
Society

CH

INN

CH

museum

SCH

EAST POULTNEY
SCALE 1:1250

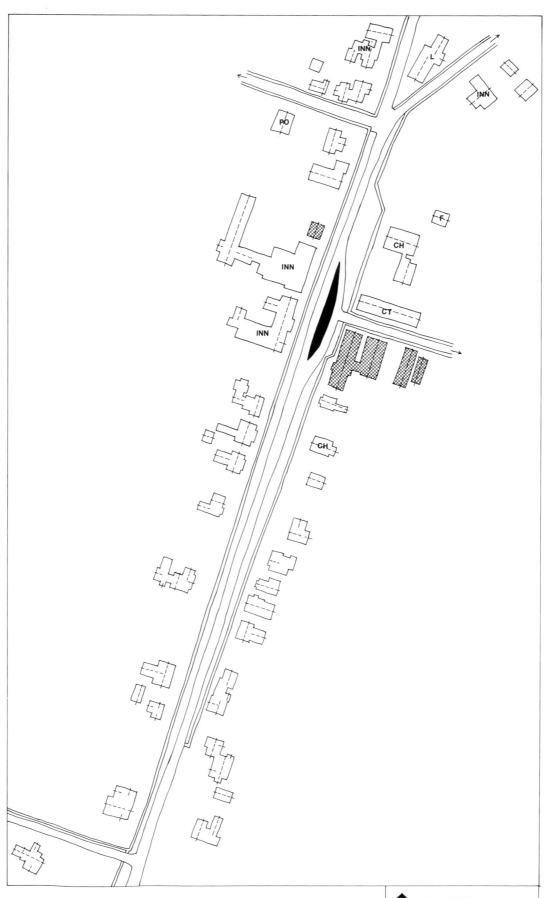

MANCHESTER
SCALE 1:1250

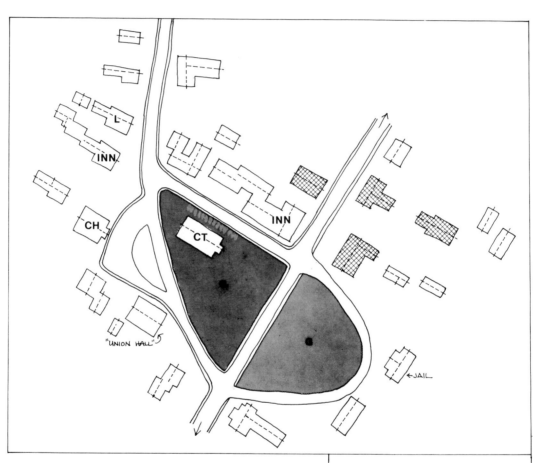

"UNION HALL"

L

INN

CH

CT

INN

JAIL

NEWFANE
SCALE 1:1250

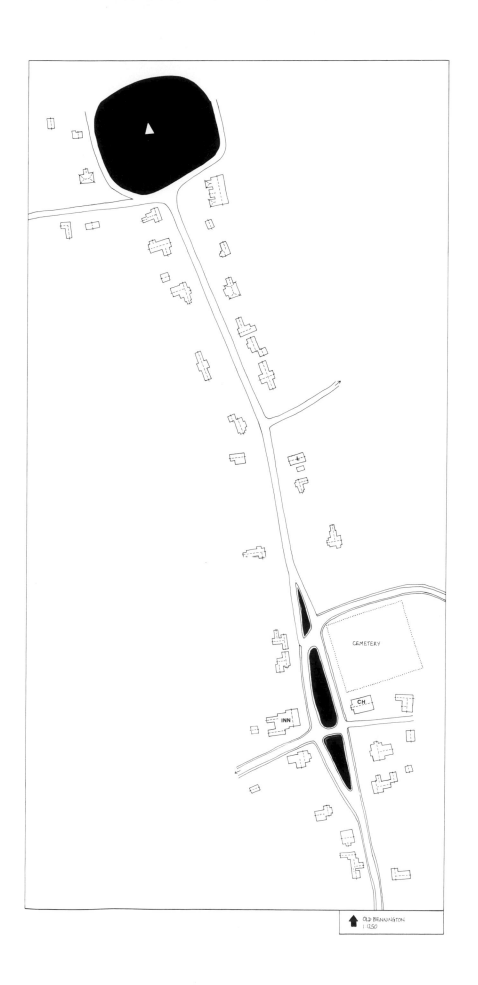

OLD BENNINGTON
1 : 1250

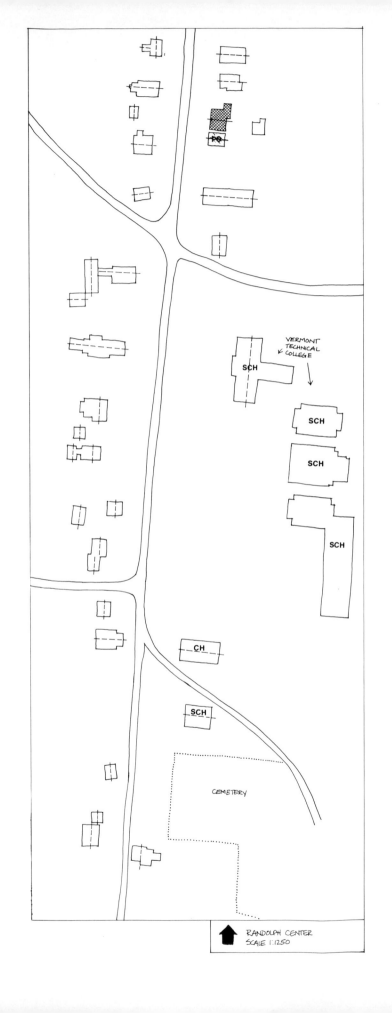

PO

VERMONT
TECHNICAL
COLLEGE

SCH

SCH

SCH

SCH

CH

SCH

CEMETERY

RANDOLPH CENTER
SCALE 1:1250

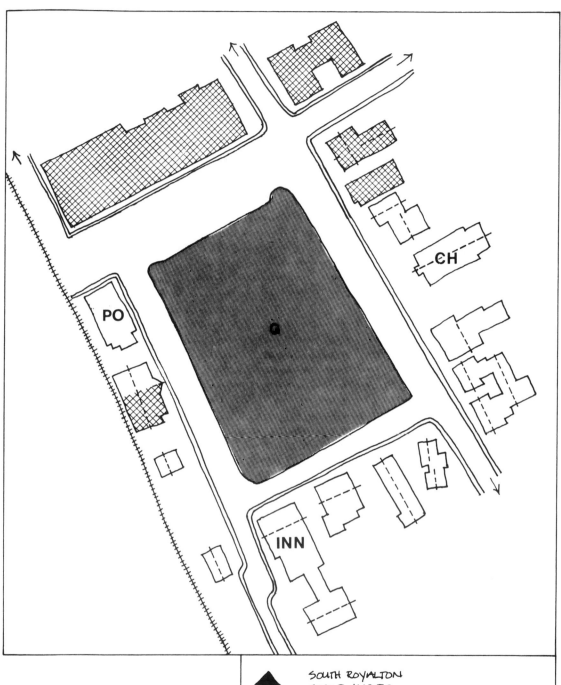

PO

CH

INN

SOUTH ROYALTON
SCALE 1:1250

STOWE
1:1250

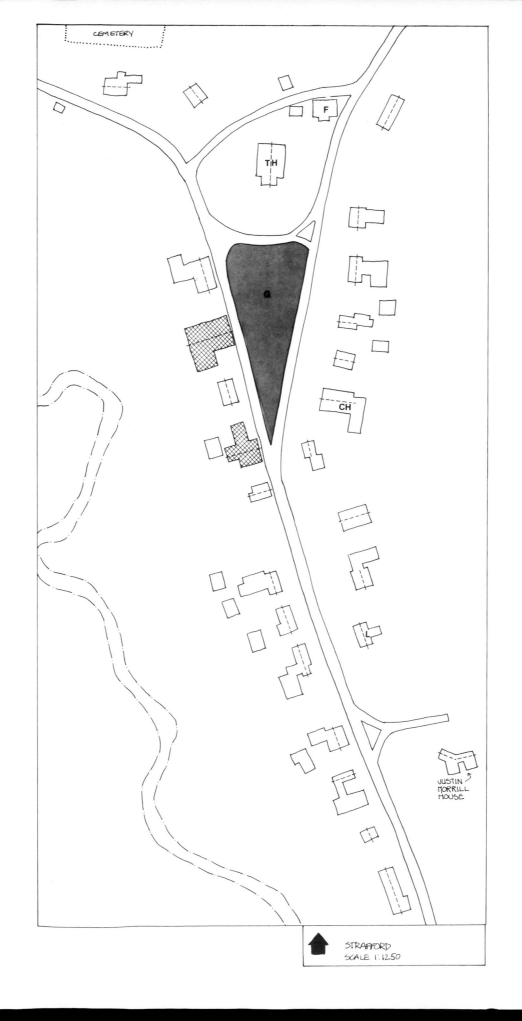

CEMETERY

F

TH

G

CH

JUSTIN
MORRILL
HOUSE

STRAFFORD
SCALE 1:1250

HEALTH
CENTER

CH

CH

PO

HISTORICAL
SOCIETY

CT

COVERED
BRIDGE

INN

TH

CH

WOODSTOCK
SCALE: 1" = 500'